Everyman's Poetry

Everyman, I will go with thee,
and be thy guide

Jonathan Swift

Selected and edited by MICHAEL BRUCE

Goldsmiths College, University of London

EVERYMAN

J. M. Dent · London

This edition first published by Everyman Paperbacks in 1998
Selection, introduction and other critical apparatus
© J. M. Dent 1998

J. M. Dent
Orion Publishing Group
Orion House
5 Upper St Martin's Lane
London WC2H 9EA

Typeset by Deltatype Ltd, Birkenhead, Merseyside
Printed in Great Britain by
The Guernsey Press Co. Ltd, Guernsey, C. I.

British Library Cataloguing-in-Publication Data
is available on request.

ISBN 0 460 87945 6

Contents

for Frank Miles

Note on the Author and Editor

When JONATHAN SWIFT was born in Dublin on 30 November, 1667, his family, of Yorkshire stock, had only been in Ireland since shortly before the Restoration of Charles II. According to Swift, his father and his uncles had been 'driven thither by their sufferings, and by the death of their father'. In the popular mind, the author of *The Drapier's Letters* and *A Modest Proposal* remains the champion of Irish causes, yet his description of the family's emigration points up his own ambiguous relationship with the land of his birth. After an education at Trinity College, Dublin, Swift lost little time in removing himself, in 1689, to England, where he became secretary to Sir William Temple. Throughout his ten years with Temple, Swift's ambitions were set on a London career, but when patronage proved to be unforthcoming he turned to the Church of Ireland as an alternative avenue of preferment. He was ordained priest in 1695, and eventually installed as Dean of St Patrick's in 1713. Between Temple's death in 1699 and a last visit to Pope in 1727, Swift was vigorously shuttling between Dublin and London. In England he found the company he sought: statesmen and writers. It was a world of power-broking, political chicanery and literary intrigue. He wrote for the Tories, and, with his fellow-authors of the Scriblerus Club (Pope, Gay, Arbuthnot, Parnell), he sustained a satirical war of attrition against the Walpole administration. Swift is best known for his prose satires – *A Tale of a Tub, Gulliver's Travels, A Modest Proposal* – but throughout his life he was also writing, although rarely publishing, in a variety of poetic genres. The tonal range is varied, but with one or two exceptions, the most indelible of Swift's verses are marked by the same obsession with peeling back the polite veneer of eighteenth-century life which is so familiar from the prose works.

MICHAEL BRUCE was born in Surrey and educated at King's College School, Wimbledon, Fitzwilliam College, Cambridge and Westfield College, London. He is now Lecturer in English Literature at

Goldsmiths College, University of London. He has published on the pastoral tradition, and on neo-classical literary theory, and has a particular interest in representations of the English countryside in eighteenth- and nineteenth-century poetry.

Chronology of Swift's Life

Chronology of his Times

Year	Age	Life
1673	6	Enters Kilkenny School
1682	15	Enters Trinity College, Dublin

Year	Literary Context	Historical Events
1674	Milton dies Herrick dies	Peace treaty with the Dutch Shaftesbury and Buckingham dismissed
1675	Wycherley, *The Country Wife*	Wren begins St Paul's Cathedral
1676	Etherege, *The Man of Mode* Wycherley, *The Plain-Dealer*	
1678	Marvell dies Bunyan, *Pilgrim's Progress*, Pt.i.	Titus Oates and the Popish Plot
1680	Butler dies John Wilmot, Earl of Rochester, dies Bunyan, *The Life and Death of Mr Badman* Burnet, *Passages of the Life and Death of the Earl of Rochester*	Monmouth progresses through the West-country
1681	Dryden, *Absalom and Achitophel* Oldham, *Satires upon the Jesuits*	Move by Shaftesbury to have Monmouth named as Charles's heir. New Exclusion Bill brought in and the King dissolves Parliament. Shaftesbury indicted for treason but acquitted by Grand Jury
1682	Bunyan, *The Holy War* Dryden, *The Medal, MacFlecknoe, Religio Laici*	Shaftesbury flees to Holland Monmouth arrested
1683	Oldham dies Walton dies	Shaftesbury dies in Holland Monmouth departs to Holland
1685	Dryden, *Threnodia Augustalis*	Charles II dies 6 February and James II succeeds Monmouth lands at Lyme Regis After defeat at Sedgemoor he is executed on 15 July The Bloody Assizes

Year	Age	Life
1686	19	Graduates BA, *speciali gratia* ('by special grace') after a chequered academic career
1689	22	Leaves Ireland and accepts the patronage of Sir William Temple. Installed at Moor Park where he meets Esther Johnson ('Stella'), then eight years old
1690	23	Advised by physicians treating symptoms of Ménière's disease to return to Ireland
1691	24	Returns to Moor Park, via Oxford, and writes his first poem, 'Ode to the King'
1692	25	Takes an MA from Hart Hall, Oxford, with a view to ordination
1694	27	To Ireland to be ordained deacon on 25 October
1695	28	Ordained priest 13 January. Presented to the Prebend of Kilroot at the end of the same month
1696	29	Returns to Moor Park and probably begins to write *A Tale of a Tub*
1699	32	Temple dies in January. In the autumn Swift visits Ireland as chaplain to the Earl of Berkeley

Year	Literary Context	Historical Events
1688	Bunyan dies Pope born Shadwell becomes Poet Laureate	Glorious Revolution. William of Orange advances from landing at Torbay. James II deposed
1689	*Poems on Affairs of State* published Samuel Richardson born	War declared on France Scottish Jacobites defeated at Killiecrankie
1690	Locke, *An Essay Concerning Human Understanding, Two Treatises of Government*	William III defeats James in Ireland at the Battle of the Boyne
1693	Congreve, *The Old Bachelor, The Double Dealer*	
1694	Voltaire born Wotton, *Reflections upon Ancient and Modern Learning*	Bank of England founded Queen Mary dies
1697	Hogarth born Dampier, *A New Voyage Round the World* Defoe, *An Essay upon Projects* Vanbrugh, *The Provoked Wife*	Treaty of Ryswick between England, France, Holland and Spain

Year	Age	Life
1700	33	Becomes Vicar of Laracor in March, and is presented to the Prebend of St Patrick's Cathedral, Dublin, in September
1701	34	Returns to England. Esther Johnson leaves to live in Ireland, shortly followed by Swift
1702	35	Awarded Doctor of Divinity from Trinity College, Dublin
1704	37	In England to publish *A Tale of a Tub*, returning to Ireland in May
1707	40	In England again representing the Irish Clergy
1708	41	Meets Addison and Steele, and Esther Vanhomrigh. Publishes *Bickerstaff Papers*
1709	42	Writes papers for Steele's *Tatler*. Returns to Ireland in the summer
1710	43	In England in September. Writes for *The Examiner* on behalf of the Tories. Begins the *Journal to Stella*
1711	44	Publishes *Miscellanies in Prose and Verse* and *The Conduct of the Allies*
1713	46	To Dublin to be appointed Dean of St Patrick's: returns to England in October. Possibly meets Pope at this time

Year	Literary Context	Historical Events
1700	Dryden dies Congreve, *The Way of the World*	
1701	Defoe, *The True-born Englishman*	Act of Settlement fixes succession on House of Hanover James II dies War of Spanish Succession begins
1702	Defoe, *Shortest Way with Dissenters*. Condemned to the pillory	William III dies and Anne becomes Queen
1704	Dennis, *Grounds of Criticism in Poetry*	Marlborough triumphs at Blenheim Gibraltar captured Newton, *Optics*
1707	Farquhar, *Beaux' Stratagem* Farquhar dies Fielding born	Union of England, Scotland and Wales as Great Britain
1709	Johnson born Pope, *Pastorals* Steele, *Tatler*	Marlborough triumphs at Malplaquet
1711	Addison, *Spectator* Pope, *Essay on Criticism* Shaftesbury, *Characteristics*	Occasional Conformity Act Marlborough dismissed
1712	Arbuthnot, *History of John Bull* Pope, *Rape of the Lock* (two-canto version)	Barrier Treaty. Negotiations at Utrecht
1713	Sterne born Steele, *Guardian* Gay, *Rural Sports* Pope, *Windsor Forest*	Treaty of Utrecht

Year	Age	Life
1714	47	Settles permanently in Ireland. Esther Vanhomrigh follows
1720	53	Attracts political censure for his publication of *A Proposal for the Universal Use of Irish Manufacture*. Possibly begins work on *Gulliver's Travels*
1723	56	Esther Vanhomrigh dies
1724	57	Publishes *The Drapier's Letters*
1726	59	Visiting Pope in England. *Gulliver's Travels* published after his return to Ireland
1727	60	To England once more, staying with Pope. This will be his last visit to England
1727–28	61	Publishes, jointly with Pope, the *Miscellanies* in two volumes
1729	62	Publishes *A Modest Proposal*

Year	Literary Context	Historical Events
1714	Gay, *Shepherd's Week* Pope, *Rape of the Lock* (five-canto version)	Queen Anne dies George I becomes King
1715	Pope, trans. of the *Iliad*	Jacobite rebellion put down
1716	Gay, *Trivia* Wycherley dies Gray born	Septennial Act, giving Parliament a life of seven instead of three years
1719	Addison dies Defoe, *Robinson Crusoe* and *Further* *Adventures*	
1721	Collins born Smollett born	Walpole made Lord Treasurer, and Chancellor of the Exchequer
1722	Parnell, *Poems on* *Several Occasions* edited by Pope Defoe, *Moll Flanders*	Marlborough dies Walpole in the ascendant
1724	Defoe, *Roxana, Tour* *through Great Britain*	Wood's Halfpence in Ireland
1725	Defoe, *Complete English* *Tradesman* Pope, trans. of the *Odyssey*	Peter the Great dies Treaty of Hanover between England, France and Prussia
1727	Dyer, *Grongar Hill* Gay, *Fables*	George I dies. George II succeeds to the throne Newton dies
1728	Gay, *Beggar's Opera* Pope, *Dunciad* (i–iii)	

Year	Age	Life
1731	64	Writing poetry: including the scatological pieces and the beginning of *Verses on the Death of Dr Swift*
1732	65	Publishes third volume of *Miscellanies*
1735	68	First four volumes of the collected works published by Faulkner
1738	71	Publishes *Polite Conversation*. Senility creeps on apace
1742	75	Adjudged to be 'of unsound mind and memory' and incapable of controlling his daily existence

Year	Literary Context	Historical Events
1730	Fielding, *Tom Thumb* Thomson, *Seasons* Goldsmith born	
1731	Defoe dies Pope, *Epistle to Burlington*	
1733	Pope, *Essay on Man* (i–iii), *Epistle to Bathurst*	Walpole's Excise Scheme
1734	Pope, *Epistle to Cobham*	
1735	Pope, *Epistle to a Lady*, *Epistle to Arbuthnot*	Copyright Act
1737	Green, *The Spleen* Shenstone, *Poems on Various Occasions*	Licensing Act subjects plays to censorship by Lord Chamberlain Queen Caroline dies Prince of Wales heads opposition
1739	Hume, *Treatise of Human Nature*	War with Spain
1740	Richardson, *Pamela*	War of Austrian Succession
1741	Arbuthnot *et al.*, *Memoirs of Scriblerus* Fielding, *Shamela*	
1742	Collins, *Persian Eclogues* Pope, *The New Dunciad* (Book IV of revised work) Young, *The Complaint, or Night Thoughts* Fielding, *Joseph Andrews*	Walpole resigns: Carteret in ministry
1743	Blair, *The Grave* Pope, *The Dunciad* (final version)	George II present at England's victory at Dettingen

Year	Age	Life
1745	78	Dies on 19 October

Year	Literary Context	Historical Events
1744	Pope dies Akenside, *The Pleasures of the Imagination*	Carteret falls: Pelham ministry France declares war on England
1745	Collins, *Odes*	Charles Edward (the Young Pretender) wins the battle of Prestonpans: he would be defeated in the following year at Culloden

Introduction

Satire has always been a nervy vocation. Apart from any threats of state oppression, libel suits, or incidents in dark alleys, the satirist is faced with the delicate task of negotiating a relationship with a reader who may be instinctively wary. It is possible for the satirist to flatter: to hint at a comradely parity of wit and discrimination, with an invitation to view the rest of the world with a sneer and a ribald disdain. Such an approach may well nudge the reader into an embarrassed recognition of kinship with the victims, but equally it is easy to glory in the discomfort of others, and resist the identification. In part, this is true of Pope, Swift's fellow poet and ironist. Certainly, in his verses, we keep good company, rubbing shoulders with the Lords Bathurst and Burlington with whom, it is implied, we share a common taste. This, however, is not Swift's way. His satire feeds off the reader's insecurity, and to this end it provokes and bemuses, misdirecting us into a landscape where the signposts have been turned, and apparently familiar footpaths have been mined with unlooked-for ambiguities.

This much will be apparent to anyone who knows Swift as a writer of prose satire. When George Faulkner published the Dublin edition of the *Works* in 1735, the text of *Gulliver's Travels* was illustrated with a portrait of Lemuel Gulliver which carried the sobriquet *Spendide Mendax* (magnificent liar). And so he proved to be: a false *ingénu*, whose word was rarely reliable, encouraging generations of critics to discover in the misanthropic Gulliver, co-habiting with his horses at the end of the final voyage, an alter-ego of Swift himself. Similar cases of mistaken identity occur, all too frequently, amongst readers of Swift's poetry: and worse, to the depressing profile of misanthrope is added the alarming identikit of a thoroughgoing misogynist.

In the more notorious of Swift's verses, the so-called 'scatological' poems, we find ourselves in recognizable territory, where it behoves us to step warily, if we wish to avoid treading in something rather unpleasant. The reader is stationed covertly behind a boudoir screen, or offered a keyhole through which to peer. The vistas of human detritus, of ordure and decrepitude through which Gulliver had wandered so laconically, have shrunk to the dimensions of a female closet; and with the narrowing focus comes an intensity that breeds ambiguities of response. But watchers at keyholes are frequently victims of partial perspectives, a fact which may be further complicated by the gender of the voyeur. This group of poems, written in the early 1730s, and verses like 'The Progress of Beauty', similar in tone but from a decade earlier, will need further scrutiny. Swift's output, however, is considerable, and it spans his writing career from the 1690s to the mid-1730s, ending just short of ten years before his death in 1745.

In 1732, when he was composing such powerfully corrosive pieces as 'The Lady's Dressing Room', Swift still felt inclined to disparage his poetic talent, and wrote to a friend: 'I have been only a man of rhymes, and that upon trifles, never having written serious couplets in my life'. To accept at face value a self-assessment of such insouciance from Swift is rarely to be recommended: a caveat of especial resonance when reading the *Verses* upon his own death which open this volume. Nevertheless some account needs to be made of those parts of his work which have been excluded from this selection. The odes and occasional poems that were written during his time as Sir William Temple's secretary resist even the most enthusiastic attempts to prise them from their particular time and place. For similar reasons, much of the political verse written throughout Swift's life proves to be more attractive to the historian than the common reader, and can claim no credible place in a short anthology. At the risk of appearing too easily dismissive, the same case is made against Swift's poems on Irish topics. His reputation as an Irish patriot is safe, but the verse treatment of such affairs remains stubbornly parochial, especially when set beside the compelling indictments of his prose satires.

From amongst the work that was spawned by contemporary politics, two poems are included which owe their place as much to their vehemence of feeling as to any historical significance. Augustan satirists, for all their claims to be advocates of moderation, are notorious for the violence of their attitudes and methods. This was never better illustrated than in Swift's prolonged vendetta against the Duke of Marlborough. The first attempted assassination, 'The Fable of Midas', found its provenance in an orchestrated Tory campaign against the greed and perceived corruption of the

Duke. It concluded in the hugely successful *Conduct of the Allies* (1711) which made no small contribution to Marlborough's dismissal at the end of that year. Just over a decade later, the conqueror of Blenheim was dead, and, although illness had kept him out of public affairs for several years, the event was 'celebrated' by Swift's 'Satirical Elegy on the Death of a Late Famous General'. In part, the poem may be voicing a party line, but the virulence of Swift's gleeful contemplation of the great man's return 'to that dirt from whence he sprung' suggests an unforgiving vein in the poet's temperament. The Duke's passing had been marked by an elegiac outpouring of national mourning: in characteristic fashion, Swift set about upending the genre, transmuting eulogy into abuse, and ensuring that even the corpse could not feel finally safe from the satirist's venom.

England's new age of Augustus consciously struck an heroic pose. Popular clichés enshrined its elegance and rationality: its self-image was assertive and confident. It comes as no surprise that the reality fell alarmingly short of the ideal, and, in the gulf that lay between, the satirists found a dark and murky subterranean world richly populated with species of clandestine low-life. In *A Tale of a Tub* the narrator promotes the 'artificial mediums, false lights, refracted angles, varnish, and tinsel', which in his view are the very substance of 'the felicity and enjoyment of mortal men': surely, he claims, there is no profit to be had from 'the art of exposing weak sides, and publishing infirmities'. But this, precisely, is the art practised by Swift. Unwilling to be deceived by veneers and painted surfaces (at least, this would appear to be the case), Swift felt compelled, sometimes obsessively, to anatomize the disease and decay that lay beneath. When the crazed spokesman of *A Tale* 'ordered the carcass of a beau to be stripped in [his] presence', Swift would have lent an eager hand. Unlike the madman, however, he would not have been amazed at discovering 'so many unsuspected faults under one suit of clothes'. One other such experiment might have stirred Swift's imagination even more powerfully. 'Last week I saw a woman flayed, and you will hardly believe, how much it altered her person for the worse'. These words, stamped with an ironic die, might serve as an epigraph for many of Swift's poems upon women, which more than any other of his verses have provoked the most extensive and excitable critical wrangling. Any debate about Swift's treatment of and attitude to women will find its

obvious locus in the 'scatological' group written between 1732 and
1734: 'The Lady's Dressing Room', 'A Beautiful Young Nymph
Going to Bed', 'Strephon and Chloe', 'Cassinus and Peter'. Such a
discussion will be faced with what appear to be a bevy of female
yahoos who have migrated to the 'polite' precincts of metropolitan
London. Women have been reduced, at least in the jaundiced
masculine eye, to a compendium of bodily functions. However, as
these urban nymphs seem to incarnate a pecular obsession on the
part of Swift, confrontation may be justifiably delayed by
considering other women who have received tribute from the poet.

Between 1719 and 1727, Swift wrote a series of birthday verses
for Esther Johnson (Stella), and towards the end of that period
published his longest poem, 'Cadenus and Vanessa', which pur-
ports to record, or perhaps more truthfully mythologize, his
friendship with Esther Vanhomrigh (Vanessa). The precise nature
of Swift's tangled relationship with his two companions, both many
years his junior, is the stuff of biography, but the range of feeling on
display offers an appealing counterbalance to the tawdry cameos of
his fictional Celias, Corinnas and Chloes. The Stella poems, in
particular, are touched by a tenderness and respect which are rare
things in the body of Swift's work. In the lines of 1727, the last to be
written before Esther Johnson's death in the January of the
following year, he offers an elegiac review of their time together,
and lingers over their touching mutual dependence. Yet even
amongst poems of such intimacy, the feelings expressed are never
wholly free of that familiar undertow of ironic banter. It may be a
wry, and not very flattering observation upon Stella's expanding
girth ('Stella's Birthday, 1719'), or it may voice a somewhat
acerbic criticism of her ill-governed temper ('To Stella, Who
Collected and Transcribed His Poems'). Despite the very apparent
affection, it is as though Swift is at pains to exclude all hints of
romantic emotion which poems of this sort might have encour-
aged. He prefers to act out a schoolmasterly role (which is equally
true of his stance in 'Cadenus and Vanessa'), thereby controlling
what could be uncomfortably revealing in lines committed to
paper. In refusing to romanticize either woman, Swift is adjusting
the focus of his poetic lens just as he will when he pries beneath the
skirts of his inner-city queans. The analogy may appear to be
outlandish, comparing Stella's middle-aged spread to the grotesque
dismemberment of 'Corinna, pride of Drury Lane', but is it in

the end simply a question of degree? It might be argued that, in one
sense, Swift does his best to idealize Stella and Vanessa, placing
them beyond the reach of carnal fantasy. His methods are curious,
but in composing their characters, Swift carefully robs them of their
sexual identities, preferring to cast them in the role of surrogate
male companions. Vanessa is endorsed for possessing qualities
which are 'for manly bosoms chiefly fit', and Stella projects a solid,
masculine reliability. As the years had passed, Swift was forced to
relinquish his early images of them as young girls: but in the poems,
at least, he could allow them to grow old in a way that suited his
ideas about them.

In the poems of the 1730s, women are not deprived of their
sexuality, although it becomes such an oozy and malodorous affair
that it certainly loses any pretensions to being erotic. They do,
however, lose their dignity, along with their understained clothes,
their cosmetic camouflage, their mouseskin eyebrows, and their
glass eyes. The fragrance that surrounds them creeps in from the
privy, and whatever female mystique they may once have
possessed soon flies out of the window on a bean-driven fart. In the
case of Corinna ('A Beautiful Young Nymph Going to Bed'), Swift
simply invites us to view the wretched disassembly of all those false
applications which are her sad attempt to reconstruct some
semblance of a long-lost beauty. We are left wondering at her
whimpering nightmares of violent punters, Bridewell jail, and
transportation to Jamaica: wondering uneasily, indeed, whether
we can afford any sympathy for such pathetic yet comic wreckage.
In the other three poems of the group, our intrusion into bedroom
and boudoir is mediated by romantically credulous husbands and
lovers. In some ways, however nauseous the vision, it was easy to
identify Corinna as a victim. With the introduction of two
Strephons and a Cassinus, we struggle to disengage ourselves from
their voyeuristic squeamishness. Surely, as mature adults (and the
temptation to add 'male' to the formulation is strong), we should be
aware that women defecate, use piss-pots, squeeze blackheads and
stain their underclothes – they are, after all, no different from men.
Yet there is a tenor of violence attached to this parade of female
physical function, which is not easily explained away. Swift may
appear to contain it in a burlesque world of 'urban pastoral', but the
images are possessed of a power that seems to spill over the literary
boundaries, contaminating the environment at large. On the

strength of this impression would we be justified in 'outing' Swift as an unreconstructed misogynist? It is probably not sufficient to reverse the argument, and knowingly suggest that what Swift really has in his sights is the average male's fatuous compulsion to idealize the objects of his romantic and sexual desire. As a proposition, it is partly true: as the final word, it is too glib.

There remains the unnerving possibility that Swift's gallery of grubby pictures is, in fact, a complaint that too much is on show. In a radical reading of this sort, the poems lament the fact that humanity lacks the ingenuity, the artifice, adequate to concealment. Faced with all the corporeal nastiness of our bodies, perhaps we would do well to retreat into the comfort of illusion. If this were the case, then Swift's frustration would be with the beauticians, the painters, and the poets who have failed to create effective fictions. Perhaps, after all, happiness does reside in a 'perpetual possession of being well deceived' (*A Tale of a Tub*): perhaps the narrator of the *Tale* was right to place his faith in 'false lights . . . varnish, and tinsel'. To arrive at such a conclusion seems perverse: but to have traced such a contradictory circle should convincingly underline how obdurately Swift resists a singular reading. And if the reader is left confused and bemused, who is to say that Swift has achieved less than he attempted?

In conclusion, some mention should be made of the ordering of the poems. As will be seen from the notes, this arrangement adopts a fairly cavalier attitude towards chronology. Poems are grouped by association: a common topic, a shared attitude, or an addressee will bring them together. Only in the opening verses and the final line has there been any artful contrivance. The volume begins with Swift's own obituary, and it ends with a plaintive cloacal refrain when one of his bathetic lovers uncovers what a recent biographer has described as 'the original sin of the chamber pot'.

MICHAEL BRUCE

Verses on the Death of Dr Swift, D.S.P.D.

Occasioned by reading the following
maxim in Rochefoucauld

*Dans l'adversité de nos meilleurs amis nous trouvons quelque chose, qui ne
nous deplaist pas.*

In the Adversity of our best Friends, we find something that doth not
displease us.

As Rochefoucauld his maxims drew
From nature, I believe 'em true:
They argue no corrupted mind
In him; the fault is in mankind.

This maxim more than all the rest
Is thought too base for human breast:
'In all distresses of our friends
We first consult our private ends,
While nature kindly bent to ease us,
Points out some circumstance to please us.'   10

If this perhaps your patience move
Let reason and experience prove.

We all behold with envious eyes,
Our equals raised above our size.

Who would not at a crowded show,
Stand high himself, keep others low?
I love my friend as well as you,
But why should he obstruct my view?
Then let me have the higher post;
Suppose it but an inch at most.   20

If, in a battle you should find,
One, whom you love of all mankind,

Had some heroic action done,
A champion killed, or trophy won;
Rather than thus be overtopped,
Would you not wish his laurels cropped?

Dear honest Ned is in the gout,
Lies racked with pain, and you without:
How patiently you hear him groan!
How glad the case is not your own!   30

What poet would not grieve to see,
His brother write as well as he?
But rather than they should excel,
Would wish his rivals all in hell.

Her end when Emulation misses,
She turns to Envy, stings and hisses:
The strongest friendship yields to pride,
Unless the odds be on our side.

Vain humankind! Fantastic race!
Thy various follies, who can trace?   40
Self-love, ambition, envy, pride,
Their empire in our hearts divide:
Give others riches, power, and station,
'Tis all on me a usurpation.
I have no title to aspire;
Yet, when you sink, I seem the higher.
In Pope I cannot read a line,
But with a sigh, I wish it mine:
When he can in one couplet fix
More sense than I can do in six: 50
It gives me such a jealous fit,
I cry, 'Pox take him, and his wit.'

I grieve to be outdone by Gay,
In my own humorous biting way.

Arbuthnot is no more my friend,
Who dares to irony pretend;

Which I was born to introduce,
Refined it first, and showed its use.

St John, as well as Pulteney knows,
That I had some repute for prose;   60
And till they drove me out of date,
Could maul a minister of state:
If they have mortified my pride,
And made me throw my pen aside;
If with such talents heaven has blest 'em,
Have I not reason to detest 'em?

To all my foes, dear fortune, send
Thy gifts, but never to my friend:
I tamely can endure the first;
But this with envy makes me burst.   70

Thus much may serve by way of proem:
Proceed we therefore to our poem.

The time is not remote, when I
Must by the course of nature die:
When I foresee my special friends,
Will try to find their private ends:
And though 'tis hardly understood,
Which way my death can do them good,
Yet thus, methinks, I hear 'em speak:
'See, how the Dean begins to break!   80
Poor gentleman, he droops apace,
You plainly find it in his face:
That old vertigo in his head,
Will never leave him, till he's dead:
Besides, his memory decays,
He recollects not what he says:
He cannot call his friends to mind;
Forgets the place where last he dined:
Plies you with stories o'er and o'er;
He told them fifty times before.   90

How does he fancy we can sit,
To hear his out-of-fashion wit?

But he takes up with younger folks,
Who for his wine will bear his jokes:
Faith! he must make his stories shorter,
Or change his comrades once a quarter:
In half the time he talks them round;
There must another set be found.

'For poetry, he's past his prime,
He takes an hour to find a rhyme: 100
His fire is out, his wit decayed,
His fancy sunk, his Muse a jade.
I'd have him throw away his pen;
But there's no talking to some men!'

And then their tenderness appears,
By adding largely to my years:
'He's older than he would be reckoned,
And well remembers Charles the Second.

'He hardly drinks a pint of wine;
And that, I doubt, is no good sign.   110
His stomach too begins to fail:
Last year we thought him strong and hale;
But now he's quite another thing;
I wish he may hold out till spring!'

Then hug themselves, and reason thus:
'It is not yet so bad with us!'

In such a case, they talk in tropes,
And by their fears express their hopes:
Some great misfortune to portend,
No enemy can match a friend.   120
With all the kindness they profess,
The merit of a lucky guess,
(When daily 'Howd'y's' come of course,
And servants answer: 'Worse and worse!')
Would please 'em better than to tell,
That, God be praised, the Dean is well.

Then he who prophesied the best,
Approves his foresight to the rest:
'You know I always feared the worst,
And often told you so at first.'   130
He'd rather choose that I should die,
Than his prediction prove a lie.
No one foretells I shall recover;
But all agree to give me over.

    Yet should some neighbour feel a pain,
Just in the parts, where I complain;
How many a message would he send?
What hearty prayers that I should mend?
Enquire what regimen I kept;
What gave me ease, and how I slept?   140
And more lament, when I was dead,
Than all the snivellers round my bed.

    My good companions, never fear,
For though you may mistake a year,
Though your prognostics run too fast,
They must be verified at last.

    Behold the fatal day arrive!
'How is the Dean?' 'He's just alive.'
Now the departing prayer is read:
'He hardly breathes.' 'The Dean is dead.'   150
Before the passing-bell begun,
The news through half the town is run.
'O, may we all for death prepare!
What has he left? And who's his heir?'
'I know no more than what the news is,
'Tis all bequeathed to public uses.'
'To public uses! There's a whim!
What had the public done for him?
Mere envy, avarice, and pride!
He gave it all. – But first he died.   160
And had the Dean, in all the nation,
No worthy friend, no poor relation?

So ready to do strangers good,
Forgetting his own flesh and blood!'

   Now Grub Street wits are all employed;
With elegies, the town is cloyed:
Some paragraph in every paper,
To curse the Dean, or bless the Drapier.

   The doctors, tender of their fame,
Wisely on me lay all the blame: 170
'We must confess his case was nice;
But he would never take advice:
Had he been ruled, for aught appears,
He might have lived these twenty years:
For, when we opened him, we found,
That all his vital parts were sound.'

   From Dublin soon to London spread,
'Tis told at court, 'the Dean is dead.'

   Kind Lady Suffolk, in the spleen,
Runs laughing up to tell the Queen.   180
The Queen, so gracious, mild, and good,
Cries, 'Is he gone? 'Tis time he should.
He's dead you say; why let him rot;
I'm glad the medals were forgot.
I promised them, I own; but when?
I only was a princess then;
But now as consort of the King,
You know 'tis quite another thing.'

   Now Chartres, at Sir Robert's levee,
Tells, with a sneer, the tidings heavy: 190
'Why, if he died without his shoes,'
(Cries Bob) 'I'm sorry for the news:
Oh, were the wretch but living still,
And in his place my good friend Will!
Or had a mitre on his head,
Provided Bolingbroke were dead!'

Now Curll his shop from rubbish drains;
Three genuine tomes of Swift's remains.
And then to make them pass the glibber,
Revised by Tibbalds, Moore, and Cibber.   200
He'll treat me as he does my betters,
Publish my will, my life, my letters:
Revive the libels born to die;
Which Pope must bear, as well as I.

Here shift the scene, to represent
How those I love, my death lament.
Poor Pope will grieve a month; and Gay
A week; and Arbuthnot a day.

St John himself will scarce forbear,
To bite his pen, and drop a tear.   210
The rest will give a shrug and cry,
'I'm sorry; but we all must die.'
Indifference clad in Wisdom's guise,
All fortitude of mind supplies:
For how can stony bowels melt,
In those who never pity felt?
When *we* are lashed, *they* kiss the rod,
Resigning to the will of God.

The fools, my juniors by a year,
Are tortured with suspense and fear;   220
Who wisely thought my age a screen,
When death approached, to stand between:
The screen removed, their hearts are trembling;
They mourn for me without dissembling.

My female friends, whose tender hearts
Have better learnt to act their parts,
Receive the news in doleful dumps:
'The Dean is dead, (*Pray, what is trumps?*)
Then Lord have mercy on his soul!
(*Ladies, I'll venture for the vole.*)   230
Six deans, they say, must bear the pall:
(*I wish I knew which king to call.*)'
'Madam, your husband will attend

The funeral of so good a friend.'
'No madam, 'tis a shocking sight,
And he's engaged tomorrow night!
My Lady Club would take it ill,
If he should fail her at quadrille.
He loved the Dean, (*I lead a heart.*)
But dearest friends, they say, must part.   240
His time was come, he ran his race;
We hope he's in a better place.'

Why do we grieve that friends should die?
No loss more easy to supply.
One year is past; a different scene!
No further mention of the Dean;
Who now, alas, no more is missed,
Than if he never did exist.
Where's now this favourite of Apollo?
Departed; and his works must follow: 250
Must undergo the common fate;
His kind of wit is out of date.
Some country squire to Lintot goes,
Inquiries for 'Swift in Verse and Prose':
Says Lintot, 'I have heard the name:
He died a year ago.' 'The same.'
He searcheth all his shop in vain.
'Sir, you may find them in Duck Lane:
I sent them with a load of books,
Last Monday to the pastry-cook's.   260
To fancy they could live a year!
I find you're but a stranger here.
The Dean was famous in his time,
And had a kind of knack at rhyme.
His way of writing now is past;
The town hath got a better taste:
I keep no antiquated stuff,
But, spick and span I have enough.
Pray, do but give me leave to show 'em;
Here's Colley Cibber's birthday poem.   270
This ode you never yet have seen,
By Stephen Duck, upon the Queen.

Then, here's a letter finely penned,
Against the *Craftsman* and his friend:
It clearly shows that all reflection
On ministers, is disaffection.
Next, here's Sir Robert's vindication,
And Mr Henley's last oration:
The hawkers have not got 'em yet,
Your Honour please to buy a set?   280

'Here's Woolston's tracts, the twelfth edition;
'Tis read by every politician:
The country members, when in town,
To all their boroughs send them down:
You never met a thing so smart;
The courtiers have them all by heart:
Those maids of honour who can read,
Are taught to use them for their creed.
The reverend author's good intention,
Hath been rewarded with a pension.   290
He does an honour to his gown,
By bravely running priestcraft down:
He shows, as sure as God's in Gloucester,
That Jesus was a grand impostor:
That all his miracles were cheats,
Performed as jugglers do their feats:
The church had never such a writer:
A shame be has not got a mitre!'

Suppose me dead; and then suppose
A club assembled at the Rose;   300
Where from discourse of this and that,
I grow the subject of their chat.
And, while they toss my name about,
With favour some, and some without,
One quite indifferent in the cause,
My character impartial draws:

'The Dean, if we believe report,
Was never ill received at court.
As for his works in verse and prose,

I own myself no judge of those: 310
Nor, can I tell what critics thought 'em;
But, this I know, all people bought 'em.
As with a moral view designed
To cure the vices of mankind:
His vein, ironically grave,
Exposed the fool, and lashed the knave:
To steal a hint was never known,
But what he writ was all his own.

   'He never thought an honour done him,
Because a duke was proud to own him: 320
Would rather slip aside, and choose
To talk with wits in dirty shoes:
Despised the fools with stars and garters,
So often seen caressing Chartres.
He never courted men in station,
Nor persons had in admiration;
Of no man's greatness was afraid,
Because he sought for no man's aid.
Though trusted long in great affairs,
He gave himself no haughty airs: 330
Without regarding private ends,
Spent all his credit for his friends;
And only chose the wise and good;
No flatterers; no allies in blood;
But succoured virtue in distress,
And seldom failed of good success;
As numbers in their hearts must own,
Who, but for him, had been unknown.

   'With princes kept a due decorum,
But never stood in awe before 'em: 340
And to her Majesty, God bless her,
Would speak as free as to her dresser,
She thought it his peculiar whim,
Nor took it ill as come from him.
He followed David's lesson just,
"*In princes never put thy trust.*"
And would you make him truly sour,

Provoke him with a slave in power.
The Irish senate, if you named,
With what impatience he declaimed!   350
Fair LIBERTY was all his cry;
For her he stood prepared to die;
For her he boldly stood alone;
For her he oft exposed his own.
Two kingdoms, just as faction led,
Had set a price upon his head;
But not a traitor could be found,
To sell him for six hundred pound.

   'Had he but spared his tongue and pen,
He might have rose like other men: 360
But power was never in his thought,
And wealth he valued not a groat:
Ingratitude he often found,
And pitied those who meant the wound:
But kept the tenor of his mind,
To merit well of humankind:
Nor made a sacrifice of those
Who still were true, to please his foes.
He laboured many a fruitless hour,
To reconcile his friends in power;   370
Saw mischief by a faction brewing,
While they pursued each other's ruin.
But finding vain was all his care,
He left the court in mere despair.

   'And, oh! how short are human schemes!
Here ended all our golden dreams.
What St John's skill in state affairs,
What Ormonde's valour, Oxford's cares,
To save their sinking country lent,
Was all destroyed by one event.   380
Too soon that precious life was ended,
On which alone our weal depended.
When up a dangerous faction starts,
With wrath and vengeance in their hearts:
By solemn league and covenant bound,
To ruin, slaughter, and confound;

To turn religion to a fable,
And make the government a Babel;
Pervert the law, disgrace the gown,
Corrupt the senate, rob the crown;   390
To sacrifice old England's glory,
And make her infamous in story.
When such a tempest shook the land,
How could unguarded Virtue stand?

'With horror, grief, despair the Dean
Beheld the dire destructive scene:
His friends in exile, or the Tower,
Himself within the frown of power;
Pursued by base envenomed pens,
Far to the land of slaves and fens;   400
A servile race in folly nursed,
Who truckle most, when treated worst.

'By innocence and resolution,
He bore continual persecution;
While numbers to preferment rose,
Whose merits were, to be his foes.
When, *ev'n his own familiar friends*,
Intent upon their private ends,
Like renegadoes now he feels,
Against him lifting up their heels.   410

'The Dean did by his pen defeat
An infamous destructive cheat;
Taught fools their interest to know,
And gave them arms to ward the blow.
Envy has owned it was his doing,
To save that helpless land from ruin,
While they who at the steerage stood,
And reaped the profit, sought his blood.

'To save them from their evil fate,
In him was held a crime of state.   420
A wicked monster on the bench,
Whose fury blood could never quench;

As vile and profligate a villain,
As modern Scroggs, or old Tresilian;
Who long all justice had discarded,
Nor feared he God, nor man regarded;
Vowed on the Dean his rage to vent,
'And make him of his zeal repent:
But Heaven his innocence defends,
The grateful people stand his friends;   430
Not strains of law, nor judge's frown,
Nor topics brought to please the crown,
Nor witness hired, nor jury picked,
Prevail to bring him in convict.

   'In exile, with a steady heart,
He spent his life's declining part;
Where folly, pride, and faction sway,
Remote from St John, Pope, and Gay.

   'His friendship's there, to few confined,
Were always of the middling kind: 440
No fools of rank, a mongrel breed,
Who fain would pass for lords indeed:
Where titles give no right or power,
And peerage is a withered flower,
He would have held it a disgrace,
If such a wretch had known his face.
On rural squires, that kingdom's bane,
He vented oft his wrath in vain:
Biennial squires, to market brought;
Who sell their souls and votes for naught;   450
The nation stripped, go joyful back,
To rob the church, their tenants rack,
Go snacks with thieves and rapparees,
And keep the peace, to pick up fees:
In every job to have a share,
A gaol or barrack to repair;
And turn the tax for public roads,
Commodious to their own abodes.

   'Perhaps I may allow the Dean
Had too much satire in his vein;   460

And seemed determined not to starve it,
Because no age could more deserve it.
Yet, malice never was his aim;
He lashed the vice but spared the name.
No individual could resent,
Where thousands equally were meant.
His satire points at no defect,
But what all mortals may correct;
For he abhorred that senseless tribe,
Who call it humour when they jibe: 470
He spared a hump or crooked nose,
Whose owners set not up for beaux.
True genuine dullness moved his pity,
Unless it offered to be witty.
Those, who their ignorance confessed,
He ne'er offended with a jest;
But laughed to hear an idiot quote,
A verse from Horace, learnt by rote.

'He knew an hundred pleasing stories,
With all the turns of Whigs and Tories: 480
Was cheerful to his dying day,
And friends would let him have his way.

'He gave the little wealth he had,
To build a house for fools and mad;
And showed by one satiric touch,
No nation wanted it so much:
That kingdom he hath left his debtor,
I wish it soon may have a better.'

Imitation of Part of the Sixth Satire of the Second Book of Horace

I often wished that I had clear
For life, six hundred pounds a year,
A handsome house to lodge a friend,
A river at my garden's end,
A terrace walk, and half a rood
Of land, set out to plant a wood.

Well, now I have all this and more,
I ask not to increase my store;
But should be perfectly content,
Could I but live on this side Trent;   10
Nor cross the Channel twice a year,
To spend six months with statesmen here.

I must by all means come to town,
'Tis for the service of the crown.
'Lewis; the Dean will be of use,
Send for him up, take no excuse.'
The toil, the danger of the seas;
Great ministers ne'er think of these;
Or let it cost five hundred pound,
No matter where the money's found;   20
It is but so much more in debt,
And that they ne'er considered yet.

'Good Mr Dean, go change your gown,
Let my Lord know you're come to town.'
I hurry me in haste away,
Not thinking it is levee day;
And find his honour in a pound,
Hemmed by a triple circle round,
Chequered with ribbons blue and green:
How should I thrust myself between?   30
Some wag observes me thus perplexed,
And, smiling, whispers to the next,

'I thought the Dean had been too proud,
To jostle here among a crowd.'
Another in a surly fit,
Tells me I have more zeal than wit,
'So eager to express your love,
You ne'er consider whom you shove,
But rudely press before a duke.'
I own, I'm pleased with this rebuke,   40
And take it kindly meant, to show
What I desire the world should know.

    I get a whisper, and withdraw,
When twenty fools I never saw
Come with petitions fairly penned,
Desiring I would stand their friend.

    This, humbly offers me his case:
That, begs my interest for a place.
A hundred other men's affairs,
Like bees are humming in my ears.   50
'Tomorrow my appeal comes on;
Without your help the cause is gone –'
'The Duke expects my Lord and you,
About some great affair, at two –'
'Put my Lord Bolingbroke in mind,
To get my warrant quickly signed:
Consider, 'tis my first request.'
Be satisfied. I'll do my best –
Then presently he falls to tease:
'You may for certain, if you please;   60
I doubt not, if his Lordship knew –
And Mr Dean, one word from you –'

    'Tis (let me see) three years and more
(October next, it will be four)
Since Harley bid me first attend,
And chose me for an humble friend;
Would take me in his coach to chat,
And question me of this and that;
As 'What's o-clock?' and 'How's the wind?'

'Whose chariot's that we left behind?'   70
Or gravely try to read the lines
Writ underneath the country signs;
Or, 'Have you nothing new today
From Pope, from Parnell or from Gay?'
Such tattle often entertains
My Lord and me as far as Staines:
As once a week we travel down
To Windsor, and again to town;
Where all that passes, *inter nos*,
Might be proclaimed at Charing Cross.   80

Yet some I know with envy swell,
Because they see me used so well:
'How think you of our friend the Dean?
I wonder what some people mean;
My Lord and he are grown so great,
Always together, *tête à tête*:
What! they admire him for his jokes? –
See but the fortune of some folks!'

There flies about a strange report
Of some express arrived at court: 90
I'm stopped by all the fools I meet,
And catechized in every street.
'You, Mr Dean, frequent the great;
Inform us, will the Emperor treat?
Or do the prints and papers lie?'
Faith, Sir, you know as much as I.

'Ah Doctor, how you love to jest!
'Tis now no secret' – I protest
'Tis one to me. 'Then, tell us, pray
When are the troops to have their pay?'   100
And though I solemnly declare
I know no more than my Lord Mayor,
They stand amazed, and think me grown
The closest mortal ever known.

Thus in a sea of folly tossed,
My choicest hours of life are lost:

Yet always wishing to retreat;
Oh, could I see my country seat!
There leaning near a gentle brook,
Sleep, or peruse some ancient book;   110
And there in sweet oblivion drown
Those cares that haunt the court and town.

A Description of the Morning

Now hardly here and there a hackney coach
Appearing, showed the ruddy morn's approach.
Now Betty from her master's bed had flown,
And softly stole to discompose her own.
The slipshod 'prentice from his master's door
Had pared the dirt, and sprinkled round the floor.
Now Moll had whirled her mop with dexterous airs,
Prepared to scrub the entry and the stairs.
The youth with broomy stumps began to trace
The kennel-edge, where wheels had worn the place.   10
The smallcoal-man was heard with cadence deep,
Till drowned in shriller notes of chimney-sweep.
Duns at his Lordship's gate began to meet;
And Brickdust Moll had screamed through half the street.
The turnkey now his flock returning sees,
Duly let out a-nights to steal for fees.
The watchful bailiffs take their silent stands,
And schoolboys lag with satchels in their hands.

A Description of a City Shower

In imitation of Virgil's Georgics

Careful observers may foretell the hour
(By sure prognostics) when to dread a shower.
While rain depends, the pensive cat gives o'er
Her frolics, and pursues her tail no more.
Returning home at night, you'll find the sink
Strike your offended sense with double stink.
If you be wise, then go not far to dine,
You spend in coach-hire more than save in wine.
A coming shower your shooting corns presage,
Old aches throb, your hollow tooth will rage: 10
Sauntering in coffee-house is Dulman seen;
He damns the climate, and complains of spleen.

  Meanwhile the South, rising with dabbled wings,
A sable cloud athwart the welkin flings,
That swilled more liquor than it could contain,
And like a drunkard gives it up again.
Brisk Susan whips her linen from the rope,
While the first drizzling shower is born aslope;
Such is that sprinkling which some careless quean
Flirts on you from her mop, but not so clean: 20
You fly, invoke the gods; then turning, stop
To rail; she singing, still whirls on her mop.
Not yet the dust had shunned the unequal strife,
But aided by the wind, fought still for life;
And wafted with its foe by violent gust,
'Twas doubtful which was rain, and which was dust.
Ah! where must needy poet seek for aid,
When dust and rain at once his coat invade?
His only coat, where dust confused with rain
Roughen the nap, and leave a mingled stain.   30

  Now in contiguous drops the flood comes down,
Threatening with deluge this devoted town.
To shops in crowds the daggled females fly,

Pretend to cheapen goods, but nothing buy.
The Templar spruce, while every spout's abroach,
Stays till 'tis fair, yet seems to call a coach.
The tucked-up seamstress walks with hasty strides,
While streams run down her oiled umbrella's sides.
Here various kinds, by various fortunes led,
Commence acquaintance underneath a shed.   40
Triumphant Tories, and desponding Whigs,
Forget their feuds, and join to save their wigs.
Boxed in a chair the beau impatient sits,
While spouts run clattering o'er the roof by fits;
And ever and anon with frightful din
The leather sounds; he trembles from within.
So when Troy chairmen bore the wooden steed,
Pregnant with Greeks, impatient to be freed;
(Those bully Greeks, who, as the moderns do,
Instead of paying chairmen, ran them through)   50
Laocoon struck the outside with his spear,
And each imprisoned hero quaked for fear.

Now from all parts the swelling kennels flow,
And bear their trophies with them as they go:
Filths of all hues, and odours, seem to tell
What street they sailed from, by the sight and smell.
They, as each torrent drives with rapid force
From Smithfield, or St Pulchre's shape their course;
And in huge confluent join at Snow Hill ridge,
Fall from the conduit prone to Holborn Bridge.   60
Sweepings from butchers' stalls, dung, guts, and blood,
Drowned puppies, stinking sprats, all drenched in mud,
Dead cats, and turnip-tops come tumbling down the flood.

Stella's Birthday (1719)

Stella this day is thirty-four,
(We shan't dispute a year or more:)
However Stella, be not troubled,
Although thy size and years are doubled,
Since first I saw thee at sixteen,
The brightest virgin on the green;
So little is thy form declined;
Made up so largely in thy mind.

Oh, would it please the gods to split
Thy beauty, size, and years, and wit!   10
No age could furnish out a pair
Of nymphs so graceful, wise, and fair:
With half the lustre of your eyes,
With half your wit, your years, and size:
And then before it grew too late,
How should I beg of gentle fate,
(That either nymph might have her swain,)
To split my worship too in twain.

Stella's Birthday (1721)

All travellers at first incline
Where'er they see the fairest sign,
And if they find the chambers neat,
And like the liquor, and the meat,
Will call again, and recommend
The Angel Inn to every friend.
What though the painting grows decayed,
The house will never lose its trade:
Nay, though the treacherous tapster Thomas
Hangs a new angel two doors from us,   10
As fine as dauber's hands can make it,

In hopes that strangers may mistake it,
We think it both a shame and sin
To quit the true old Angel Inn.

Now, this is Stella's case in fact,
An angel's face, a little cracked;
(Could poets, or could painters fix
How angels look at thirty-six:)
This drew us in at first, to find
In such a form an angel's mind;   20
And every virtue now supplies
The fainting rays of Stella's eyes.
See at her levee crowding swains,
Whom Stella freely entertains
With breeding, humour, wit, and sense,
And puts them to so small expense:
Their minds so plentifully fills,
And makes such reasonable bills,
So little gets for what she gives,
We really wonder how she lives!   30
And had her stock been less, no doubt
She must have long ago run out.

Then who can think we'll quit the place
When Doll hangs out a newer face;
Nailed to her window full in sight
All Christian people to invite;
Or stop and light at Chloe's head,
With scraps and leavings to be fed.

Then Chloe, still go on to prate
Of thirty-six, and thirty-eight;
Pursue your trade of scandal-picking,
Your hints that Stella is no chicken;   40
Your innuendos, when you tell us
That Stella loves to talk with fellows:
But let me warn you to believe
A truth, for which your soul should grieve;
That, should you live to see the day
When Stella's locks must all be grey,

When age must print a furrowed trace
On every feature of her face;
Though you, and all your senseless tribe,
Could art, or time, or nature bribe,   50
To make you look like Beauty's Queen,
And hold forever at fifteen:
No bloom of youth can ever blind
The cracks and wrinkles of your mind;
All men of sense will pass your door,
And crowd to Stella's at fourscore.

Stella's Birthday (1723)

A Great Bottle of Wine, Long Buried, Being That Day Dug Up

Resolved my annual verse to pay,
By duty bound, on Stella's day,
Furnished with papers, pen, and ink,
I gravely sat me down to think:
I bit my nails, and scratched my head,
But found my wit and fancy fled:
Or, if with more than usual pain,
A thought came slowly from my brain,
It cost me Lord knows how much time
To shape it into sense and rhyme: 10
And, what was yet a greater curse,
Long-thinking made my fancy worse.

    Forsaken by the inspiring Nine,
I waited at Apollo's shrine;
I told him what the world would say
If Stella were unsung today;
How I should hide my head for shame,
When both the Jacks and Robin came;
How Ford would frown, how Jim would leer;

How Sheridan the rogue would sneer,   20
And swear it does not always follow,
That '*Semel'n anno ridet Apollo.*'
I have assured them twenty times,
That Phoebus helped me in my rhymes;
Phoebus inspired me from above,
And he and I were hand in glove.
But finding me so dull and dry since,
They'll call it all poetic licence;
And when I brag of aid divine,
Think Eusden's right as good as mine.   30

    Nor do I ask for Stella's sake;
'Tis my own credit lies at stake.
And Stella will be sung, while I
Can only be a stander-by.

    Apollo, having thought a little,
Returned this answer to a tittle.

    'Though you should live like old Methusalem,
I furnish hints, and you should use all 'em,
You yearly sing as she grows old,
You'd leave her virtues half untold.   40
But, to say truth, such dullness reigns
Through the whole set of Irish deans,
I'm daily stunned with such a medley,
Dean White, Dean Daniel, and Dean Smedley;
That, let what dean soever come,
My orders are, I'm not at home;
And if your voice had not been loud,
You must have passed among the crowd.

    'But now, your danger to prevent,
You must apply to Mrs Brent,   50
For she, as priestess, knows the rites
Wherein the god of Earth delights.
First, nine ways looking, let her stand
With an old poker in her hand;
Let her describe a circle round

In Saunders' cellar on the ground:
A spade let prudent Archy hold,
And with discretion dig the mould:
Let Stella look with watchful eye,
Rebecca, Ford, and Grattans by.   60

    'Behold the bottle, where it lies
With neck elated towards the skies!
The God of Winds and God of Fire
Did to its wondrous birth conspire;
And Bacchus for the poet's use
Poured in a strong inspiring juice.
See! as you raise it from its tomb,
It drags behind a spacious womb,
And in the spacious womb contains
A sovereign medicine for the brains.   70

    'You'll find it soon, if fate consents;
If not, a thousand Mrs Brents,
Ten thousand Archys, armed with spades,
May dig in vain to Pluto's shades.

    'From thence a plenteous draught infuse,
And boldly then invoke the Muse:
(But first let Robert, on his knees,
With caution drain it from the lees)
The Muse will at your call appear,
With Stella's praise to crown the year.'   80

Stella's Birthday (1725)

As, when a beauteous nymph decays,
We say, she's past her dancing days;
So poets lose their feet by time,
And can no longer dance in rhyme.
Your annual bard had rather chose

To celebrate your birth in prose:
Yet merry folks, who want by chance
A pair to make a country dance,
Call the old housekeeper, and get her
To fill a place, for want of better: 10
While Sheridan is off the hooks,
And friend Delany at his books,
That Stella may avoid disgrace,
Once more the Dean supplies their place.

     Beauty and wit, too sad a truth!
Have always been confined to youth;
The God of Wit, and Beauty's Queen,
He twenty-one, and she fifteen:
No poet ever sweetly sung,
Unless he were like Phoebus, young;   20
Nor ever nymph inspired to rhyme,
Unless, like Venus, in her prime.
At fifty-six, if this be true,
Am I a poet fit for you?
Or at the age of forty-three,
Are you a subject fit for me?
Adieu! bright wit, and radiant eyes;
You must be grave, and I be wise.
Our fate in vain we would oppose,
But I'll be still your friend in prose: 30
Esteem and friendship to express,
Will not require poetic dress;
And if the Muse deny her aid
To have them *sung*, they may be *said*.

     But, Stella say, what evil tongue
Reports you are no longer young?
That Time sits with his scythe to mow
Where erst sat Cupid with his bow;
That half your locks are turned to grey?
I'll ne'er believe a word they say.   40
'Tis true, but let it not be known,
My eyes are somewhat dimmish grown;

For nature, always in the right,
To your decays adapts my sight,
And wrinkles undistinguished pass,
For I'm ashamed to use a glass;
And till I see them with these eyes,
Whoever says you have them, lies.

   No length of time can make you quit
Honour and virtue, sense and wit;   50
Thus you may still be young to me,
While I can better *hear* than *see*.
Oh, ne'er may Fortune show her spite,
To make me *deaf*, and mend my *sight*!

Stella's Birthday (1727)

   This day, whate'er the Fates decree,
Shall still be kept with joy by me:
This day then, let us not be told,
That you are sick, and I grown old;
Nor think on our approaching ills,
And talk of spectacles and pills;
Tomorrow will be time enough
To hear such mortifying stuff.
Yet, since from reason may be brought
A better and more pleasing thought,   10
Which can in spite of all decays,
Support a few remaining days:
From not the gravest of divines,
Accept for once some serious lines.

   Although we now can form no more
Long schemes of life, as heretofore;
Yet you, while time is running fast,
Can look with joy on what is past.

Were future happiness and pain,
A mere contrivance of the brain,   20
As atheists argue, to entice,
And fit their proselytes for vice;
(The only comfort they propose,
To have companions in their woes.)
Grant this the case, yet sure 'tis hard,
That virtue, styled its own reward,
And by all sages understood
To be the chief of human good,
Should acting, die; nor leave behind
Some lasting pleasure in the mind;   30
Which, by remembrance, will assuage,
Grief, sickness, poverty, and age;
And strongly shoot a radiant dart,
To shine through life's declining part.

Say, Stella, feel you no content,
Reflecting on a life well spent?
Your skilful hand employed to save
Despairing wretches from the grave;
And then supporting with your store,
Those whom you dragged from death before: 40
(So Providence on mortals waits,
Preserving what it first creates)
Your generous boldness to defend
An innocent and absent friend;
That courage which can make you just,
To merit humbled in the dust:
The detestation you express
For vice in all its glittering dress:
That patience under torturing pain,
Where stubborn Stoics would complain.   50

Must these, like empty shadows pass,
Or forms reflected from a glass?
Or mere chimeras in the mind,
That fly, and leave no marks behind?
Does not the body thrive and grow
By food of twenty years ago?

And, had it not been still supplied,
It must a thousand times have died.
Then, who with reason can maintain,
That no effects of food remain?   60
And, is not virtue in mankind
That nutriment that feeds the mind?
Upheld by each good action past,
And still continued by the last?
Then, who with reason can pretend,
That all effects of virtue end?

  Believe me Stella, when you show
That true contempt for things below,
Nor prize your life for other ends
Than merely to oblige your friends;   70
Your former actions claim their part,
And join to fortify your heart.
For Virtue in her daily race,
Like Janus, bears a double face;
Looks back with joy where she has gone,
And therefore goes with courage on.
She at your sickly couch will wait,
And guide you to a better state.

  O then, whatever heaven intends,
Take pity on your pitying friends!   80
Nor let your ills affect your mind,
To fancy they can be unkind.
Me, surely me, you ought to spare,
Who gladly would your sufferings share;
Or give my scrap of life to you,
And think it far beneath your due;
You, to whose care so oft I owe,
That I'm alive to tell you so.

To Stella, Who Collected
and Transcribed His Poems

As when a lofty pile is raised,
We never hear the workmen praised,
Who bring the lime, or place the stones;
But all admire Inigo Jones:
So, if this pile of scattered rhymes
Should be approved in after-times,
If it both pleases and endures,
The merit and the praise are yours.

Thou, Stella, wert no longer young,
When first for thee my harp I strung,   10
Without one word of Cupid's darts,
Of killing eyes, or bleeding hearts:
With friendship and esteem possessed,
I ne'er admitted Love a guest.

In all the habitudes of life,
The friend, the mistress, and the wife,
Variety we still pursue,
In pleasure seek for something new:
Or else, comparing with the rest,
Take comfort, that our own is best: 20
(The best we value by the worst,
As tradesmen show their trash at first:)
But his pursuits are at an end,
Whom Stella chooses for a friend.

A poet, starving in a garret,
Conning old topics like a parrot,
Invokes his mistress and his Muse,
And stays at home for want of shoes:
Should but his Muse descending drop
A slice of bread, and mutton-chop;   30
Or kindly, when his credit's out,
Surprise him with a pint of stout;

Or patch his broken stocking soles,
Or send him in a peck of coals;
Exalted in his mighty mind
He flies, and leaves the stars behind;
Counts all his labours amply paid,
Adores her for the timely aid.

Or should a porter make inquiries
For Chloe, Sylvia, Phyllis, Iris;   40
Be told the lodging, lane, and sign,
The bowers that hold those nymphs divine;
Fair Chloe would perhaps be found
With footmen tippling underground;
The charming Sylvia beating flax,
Her shoulders marked with bloody tracks;
Bright Phyllis mending ragged smocks;
And radiant Iris in the pox.

These are the goddeses enrolled
In Curll's collections, new and old,   50
Whose scoundrel fathers would not know 'em,
If they should meet 'em in a poem.

True poets can depress and raise,
Are lords of infamy and praise:
They are not scurrilous in satire,
Not will in panegyric flatter.
Unjustly poets we asperse;
Truth shines the brighter, clad in verse;
And all the fictions they pursue,
Do but insinuate what is true.   60

Now, should my praises owe their truth
To beauty, dress, or paint, or youth,
What Stoics call *without our power*,
They could not be insured an hour:
'Twere grafting on an annual stock,
That must our expectation mock,
And making one luxuriant shoot,

Die the next year for want of root:
Before I could my verses bring,
Perhaps you're quite another thing.   70

So Maevius, when he drained his skull
To celebrate some suburb trull;
His similes in order set,
And every crambo he could get;
Had gone through all the commonplaces
Worn out by wits who rhyme on faces;
Before he could his poem close,
The lovely nymph had lost her nose.

Your virtues safely I commend;
They on no accidents depend: 80
Let Malice look with all her eyes,
She dare not say the poet lies.

Stella, when you these lines transcribe,
Lest you should take them for a bribe,
Resolved to mortify your pride,
I'll here expose your weaker side.

Your spirits kindle to a flame,
Moved with the lightest touch of blame;
And when a friend in kindness tries
To show you where your error lies,   90
Conviction does but more incense;
Perverseness is your whole defence:
Truth, judgement, wit, give place to spite,
Regardless both of wrong and right.
Your virtues, all suspended, wait
Till time hath opened reason's gate:
And what is worse, your passion bends
Its force against your nearest friends;
Which manners, decency, and pride,
Have taught you from the world to hide: 100
In vain; for see, your friend hath brought
To public light your only fault;

And yet a fault we often find
Mixed in a noble, generous mind;
And may compare to Etna's fire,
Which, though with trembling, all admire;
The heat that make the summit glow,
Enriching all the vales below.
Those who, in warmer climes, complain
From Phoebus' rays they suffer pain,   110
Must own, that pain is largely paid
By generous wines beneath a shade.

Yet when I find your passions rise,
And anger sparkling in your eyes,
I grieve those spirits should be spent,
For nobler ends by nature meant.
One passion, with a different turn,
Makes wit inflame, or anger burn:
So the sun's heat, by different powers,
Ripens the grape, the liquor sours.   120
Thus Ajax, when with rage possessed,
By Pallas breathed into his breast,
His valour would no more employ,
Which might alone have conquered Troy;
But blinded by resentment, seeks
For vengeance on his friends the Greeks.

You think this turbulence of blood
From stagnating preserves the flood;
Which, thus fermenting by degrees,
Exalts the spirits, sinks the lees.   130

Stella, for once you reason wrong;
For should this ferment last too long,
By time subsiding, you may find
Nothing but acid left behind.
From passion you may then be freed,
When peevishness and spleen succeed.

Say, Stella, when you copy next,
Will you keep strictly to the text?

Dare you let these reproaches stand,
And to your failing set your hand?   140
Or if these lines your anger fire,
Shall they in baser flames expire?
Whene'er they burn, if burn they must,
They'll prove my accusation just.

Cadenus and Vanessa

Written at Windsor 1713

The shepherds and the nymphs were seen
Pleading before the Cyprian Queen.
The counsel for the fair began,
Accusing that false creature, Man.

The brief with weighty crimes was charged,
On which the pleader much enlarged;
That Cupid now has lost his art,
Or blunts the point of every dart;
His altar now no longer smokes,
His mother's aid no youth invokes: 10
This tempts freethinkers to refine,
And bring in doubt their power divine;
Now love is dwindled to intrigue,
And marriage grown a money-league.
Which crimes aforesaid (with her leave)
Were (as he humbly did conceive)
Against our sovereign lady's peace,
Against the statute in that case,
Against her dignity and crown:
Then prayed an answer, and sat down.   20

The nymphs with scorn beheld their foes;
When the defendant's counsel rose,
And, what no lawyer ever lacked,

With impudence owned all the fact:
But, what the gentlest heart would vex,
Laid all the fault on t'other sex.
That modern love is no such thing
As what those ancient poets sing:
A fire celestial, chaste, refined,
Conceived and kindled in the mind;   30
Which having found an equal flame,
Unites, and both become the same,
In different breasts together burn,
Together both to ashes turn.
But women now feel no such fire,
And only know the gross desire:
Their passions move in lower spheres,
Where'er caprice or folly steers:
A dog, a parrot, or an ape,
Or some worse brute in human shape,   40
Engross the fancies of the fair,
The few soft moments they can spare,
From visits to receive and pay;
From scandal, politics, and play,
From fans and flounces, and brocades,
From equipage and Park parades,
From all the thousand female toys,
From every trifle that employs
The out or inside of their heads,
Between their toilets and their beds.   50

    In a dull stream, which moving slow
You hardly see the current flow,
If a small breeze obstructs the course,
It whirls about for want of force,
And in its narrow circle gathers
Nothing but chaff, and straws, and feathers:
The current of a female mind
Stops thus, and turns with every wind;
Thus whirling round, together draws
Fools, fops, and rakes, for chaff and straws.   60
Hence we conclude, no women's hearts
Are won by virtue, wit, and parts:

Nor are the men of sense to blame,
For breasts incapable of flame;
The fault must on the nymphs be placed,
Grown so corrupted in their taste.

    The pleader having spoke his best,
Had witness ready to attest,
Who fairly could on oath depose,
When questions on the fact arose,   70
That every article was true;
Nor further those deponents knew:
Therefore he humbly would insist,
The bill might be with costs dismissed.

    The cause appeared of so much weight,
That Venus, from her judgement-seat,
Desired them not to talk so loud,
Else she must interpose a cloud:
For if the heavenly folks should know
These pleadings in the courts below,   80
That mortals here disdain to love,
She ne'er could show her face above.
For gods, their betters, are too wise
To value that which men despise:
'And then,' said she, 'my son and I
Must stroll in air, 'twixt land and sky;
Or else, shut out from heaven and earth,
Fly to the sea, my place of birth:
There live with daggled mermaids pent,
And keep on fish perpetual Lent.'   90

    But since the case appeared so nice,
She thought it best to take advice.
The Muses, by their King's permission,
Though foes to love, attend the session;
And on the right hand took their places
In order; on the left, the Graces:
To whom she might her doubts propose
On all emergencies that rose.

The Muses oft were seen to frown;
The Graces half ashamed looked down;   100
And 'twas observed, there were but few
Of either sex, among the crew,
Whom she or her assessors knew.
The goddess soon began to see
Things were not ripe for a decree,
And said, she must consult her books,
The lovers' *Fleta*'s, Bractons, Cokes.
First to a dapper clerk she beckoned,
To turn to Ovid, book the second;
She then referred them to a place   110
In Virgil (*vide* Dido's case):
As for Tibullus's reports,
They never passed for laws in courts;
For Cowley's briefs, and pleas of Waller,
Still their authority was smaller.

There was on both sides much to say:
She'd hear the cause another day;
And so she did; and then a third:
She heard it – there she kept her word:
But with rejoinders and replies,   120
Long bills, and answers stuffed with lies;
Demur, imparlance, and essoign,
The parties ne'er could issue join:
For sixteen years the cause was spun,
And then stood where it first begun.

Now, gentle Clio, sing or say,
What Venus meant by this delay.
The goddess much perplexed in mind,
To see her empire thus declined,
When first this grand debate arose,   130
Above her wisdom to compose,
Conceived a project in her head,
To work her ends; which, if it sped,
Would show the merits of the cause,
Far better than consulting laws.

In a glad hour Lucina's aid
Produced on earth a wondrous maid,
On whom the Queen of Love was bent
To try a new experiment.
She threw her law-books on the shelf,   140
And thus debated with herself.

'Since men allege, they ne'er can find
Those beauties in a female mind,
Which raise a flame that will endure
For ever uncorrupt and pure;
If 'tis with reason they complain,
This infant shall restore my reign.
I'll search where every virtue dwells,
From courts inclusive down to cells,
What preachers talk, or sages write,   150
These I will gather and unite,
And represent them to mankind
Collected in that infant's mind.'

This said, she plucks in heaven's high bowers
A sprig of amaranthine flowers,
In nectar thrice infuses bays,
Three times refined in Titan's rays:
Then calls the Graces to her aid,
And sprinkles thrice the new-born maid:
From whence the tender skin assumes   160
A sweetness above all perfumes;
From whence a cleanliness remains,
Incapable of outward stains;
From whence that decency of mind,
So lovely in the female kind,
Where not one careless thought intrudes,
Less modest than the speech of prudes;
Where never blush was called in aid;
That spurious virtue in a maid;
A virtue but at second-hand;   170
They blush because they understand.

The Graces next would act their part,
And showed but little of their art;

Their work was half already done,
The child with native beauty shone;
The outward form no help required:
Each breathing on her thrice, inspired
That gentle, soft, engaging air,
Which, in old times, adorned the fair;
And said, 'Vanessa be the name,   180
By which thou shalt be known to fame:
Vanessa, by the gods enrolled:
Her name on earth – shall not be told.'

But still the work was not complete;
When Venus thought on a deceit.
Drawn by her doves, away she flies,
And finds out Pallas in the skies:
'Dear Pallas, I have been this morn
To see a lovely infant born:
A boy in yonder isle below,   190
So like my own, without his bow:
By beauty could your heart be won,
You'd swear it is Apollo's son;
But it shall ne'er be said, a child
So hopeful, has by me been spoiled:
I have enough besides to spare,
And give him wholly to your care.'

Wisdom's above suspecting wiles:
The Queen of Learning gravely smiles;
Down from Olympus comes with joy,   200
Mistakes Vanessa for a boy;
Then sows within her tender mind
Seeds long unknown to womankind,
For manly bosoms chiefly fit,
The seeds of knowledge, judgement, wit.
Her soul was suddenly endued
With justice, truth and fortitude;
With honour, which no breath can stain,
Which malice must attack in vain;
With open heart and bounteous hand.   210
But Pallas here was at a stand;

She knew in our degenerate days,
Bare virtue could not live on praise;
That meat must be with money bought;
She therefore, upon second thought,
Infused, yet as it were by stealth,
Some small regard for state and wealth:
Of which, as she grew up, there stayed
A tincture in the prudent maid:
She managed her estate with care,   220
Yet liked three footmen to her chair.
But lest he should neglect his studies
Like a young heir, the thrifty goddess
(For fear young master should be spoiled)
Would use him like a younger child;
And, after long computing, found
'Twould come to just five thousand pound.

The Queen of Love was pleased, and proud,
To see Vanessa thus endowed:
She doubted not but such a dame   230
Through every breast would dart a flame;
That every rich and lordly swain
With pride would drag about her chain;
That scholars would foresake their books
To study bright Vanessa's looks:
As she advanced, that womankind
Would by her model form their mind,
And all their conduct would be tried
By her, as an unerring guide.
Offending daughters oft would hear   240
Vanessa's praise rung in their ear:
Miss Betty, when she does a fault,
Lets fall a knife, or spills the salt,
Will thus be by her mother chid,
''Tis what Vanessa never did!'
'Thus by the nymphs and swains adored,
My power shall be again restored,
And happy lovers bless my reign –'
So Venus hoped, but hoped in vain.

For when in time the Martial Maid   250
Found out the trick that Venus played.
She shakes her helm, she knits her brows,
And, fired with indignation, vows,
Tomorrow, ere the setting sun,
She'd all undo that she had done.

But in the poets we may find,
A wholesome law, time out of mind,
Had been confirmed by Fate's decree,
That gods, of whatso'er degree,
Resume not what themselves have given,   260
Or any brother god in heaven:
Which keeps the peace among the gods,
Or they must always be at odds.
And Pallas, if she broke the laws,
Must yield her foe the stronger cause;
A shame to one so much adored
For wisdom, at Jove's council-board.
Besides, she feared, the Queen of Love
Would meet with better friends above.
And though she must with grief reflect,   270
To see a mortal virgin decked
With graces, hitherto unknown
To female breasts, except her own;
Yet she would act as best became
A goddess of unspotted fame.
She knew, by augury divine,
Venus would fail in her design:
She studied well the point, and found
Her foe's conclusions were not sound,
From premises erroneous brought,   280
And therefore the deductions nought,
And must have contrary effects,
To what her treacherous foe expects.

In proper season Pallas meets
The Queen of Love, whom thus she greets
(For gods, we are by Homer told,
Can in celestial language scold):

'Perfidious goddess! but in vain
You formed this project in your brain;
A project for thy talents fit,   290
With much deceit and little wit.
Thou hast, as thou shalt quickly see,
Deceived thyself, instead of me;
For how can heavenly wisdom prove
An instrument to earthly love?
Knowst thou not yet that men commence
Thy votaries, for want of sense?
Nor shall Vanessa be the theme
To manage thy abortive scheme;
She'll prove the greatest of thy foes: 300
And yet I scorn to interpose,
But using neither skill, nor force,
Leave all things to their natural course.'

The goddess thus pronounced her doom:
When, lo! Vanessa in her bloom,
Advanced like Atalanta's star
But rarely seen, and seen from far:
In a new world with caution stepped,
Watched all the company she kept,
Well knowing, from the books she read,   310
What dangerous paths young virgins tread;
Would seldom at the Park appear,
Nor saw the playhouse twice a year;
Yet not incurious, was inclined
To know the converse of mankind.

First issued from perfumers' shops
A crowd of fashionable fops;
They asked her, how she liked the play,
Then told the tattle of the day;
A duel fought last night at two,   320
About a Lady – you know who;
Mentioned a new Italian, come
Either from Muscovy or Rome;
Gave hints of who and who's together;
Then fell to talking of the weather:

'Last night was so extremely fine,
The ladies walked till after nine.'
Then, in soft voice and speech absurd,
With nonsense every second word,
With fustian from exploded plays,   330
They celebrate her beauty's praise,
Run o'er their cant of stupid lies,
And tell the murders of her eyes.

   With silent scorn Vanessa sat,
Scarce listening to their idle chat;
Further than sometimes by a frown,
When they grew pert, to pull them down.
At last she spitefully was bent
To try their wisdom's full extent;
And said, she valued nothing less   340
Than titles, figure, shape, and dress;
That merit should be chiefly placed
In judgement, knowledge, wit, and taste;
And these, she offered to dispute,
Alone distinguished man from brute:
That, present times have no pretence
To virtue, in the noble sense,
By Greeks and Romans understood,
To perish for our country's good.
She named the ancient heroes round,   350
Explained for what they were renowned;
Then spoke with censure, or applause,
Of foreign customs, rites, and laws;
Through nature, and through art she ranged,
And gracefully her subjects changed:
In vain! her hearers had no share
In all she spoke, except to stare.
Their judgement was, upon the whole,
'That lady is the dullest soul!' –
Then tapped their forehead in a jeer,   360
As who should say – 'she wants it here!
She may be handsome, young and rich,
But none will burn her for a witch!'

A party next of glittering dames,
From round the purlieus of St James,
Came early, out of pure good will,
To catch the girl in dishabille.
Their clamour, lighting from their chairs,
Grew louder, all the way upstairs;
At entrance loudest, where they found   370
The room with volumes littered round.
Vanessa held Montaigne, and read,
Whilst Mrs Susan combed her head.
They called for tea and chocolate,
And fell into their usual chat,
Discoursing with important face,
On ribbons, fans, and gloves and lace;
Showed patterns just from India brought,
And gravely asked her what she thought,
Whether the red or green were best,   380
And what they cost? Vanessa guessed,
As came into her fancy first,
Named half the rates, and liked the worst.
To scandal next – 'What awkward thing
Was that, last Sunday, in the Ring?'
– 'I'm sorry Mopsa breaks so fast;
I said her face would never last.'
'Corinna, with that youthful air,
Is thirty, and a bit to spare.
Her fondness for a certain earl   390
Began when I was but a girl!'
'Phyllis, who but a month ago
Was married to the Tunbridge beau,
I saw coquetting t'other night
In public with that odious knight!'

They rallied next Vanessa's dress:
'That gown was made for old Queen Bess.'
'Dear madam, let me set your head:
Don't you intend to put on red?'
'A petticoat without a hoop!   400
Sure, you are not ashamed to stoop!

With handsome garters at your knees,
No matter what a fellow sees.'

    Filled with disdain, with rage inflamed,
Both of her self and sex ashamed,
The nymph stood silent out of spite,
Nor would vouchsafe to set them right.
Away the fair detractors went,
And gave, by turns, their censures vent.
'She's not so handsome, in my eyes: 410
For wit, I wonder where it lies!'
'She's fair and clean, and that's the most;
But why proclaim her for a toast?'
'A babyface; no life, no airs,
But what she learnt at country fairs;
Scarce knows what difference is between
Rich Flanders lace, and Colbertine.
I'll undertake my little Nancy
In flounces has a better fancy.'
'With all her wit, I would not ask   420
Her judgement, how to buy a mask.'
'We begged her but to patch her face,
She never hit one proper place;
Which every girl at five years old
Can do as soon as she is told.'
'I own, that out-of-fashion stuff
Becomes the creature well enough.'
'The girl might pass, if we could get her
To know the world a little better.'
(*To know the world*! a modern phrase,   430
For visits, ombre, balls and plays.)

    Thus, to the world's perpetual shame,
The Queen of Beauty lost her aim.
Too late with grief she understood,
Pallas had done more harm than good;
For great examples are but vain,
Where ignorance begets disdain.
Both sexes, armed with guilt and spite,
Against Vanessa's power unite;
To copy her, few nymphs aspired;   440

Her virtues fewer swains admired.
So stars beyond a certain height
Give mortals neither heat nor light.

   Yet some of either sex, endowed
With gifts superior to the crowd,
With virtue, knowledge, taste and wit,
She condescended to admit:
With pleasing arts she could reduce
Men's talents to their proper use;
And with address each genius held   450
To that wherein it most excelled;
Thus making others' wisdom known,
Could please them, and improve her own.
A modest youth said something new,
She placed it in the strongest view.
All humble worth she strove to raise,
Would not be praised, yet loved to praise.
The learned met with free approach,
Although they came not in a coach:
Some clergy too she would allow,   460
Nor quarrelled at their awkward bow;
But this was for Cadenus' sake,
A gownman of a different make;
Whom Pallas, once Vanessa's tutor,
Had fixed on for her coadjutor.

   But Cupid, full of mischief, longs
To vindicate his mother's wrongs.
On Pallas all attempts are vain:
One way he knows to give her pain;
Vows, on Vanessa's heart to take   470
Due vengeance, for her patron's sake.
Those early seeds by Venus sown,
In spite of Pallas, now were grown;
And Cupid hoped they would improve
By time, and ripen into love.
The boy made use of all his craft,
In vain discharging many a shaft,
Pointed at colonels, lords, and beaux:

Cadenus warded off the blows;
For placing still some book betwixt,   480
The darts were in the cover fixed,
Or often blunted and recoiled,
On Plutarch's *Morals* struck, were spoiled.

    The Queen of Wisdom could foresee,
But not prevent the Fates' decree;
And human caution tries in vain
To break that adamantine chain.
Vanessa, though by Pallas taught,
By Love invulnerable thought,
Searching in books for wisdom's aid,   490
Was, in the very search, betrayed.

    Cupid, though all his darts were lost,
Yet still resolved to spare no cost:
He could not answer to his fame
The triumphs of that stubborn dame,
A nymph so hard to be subdued,
Who neither was coquette nor prude.
'I find,' said he, 'she wants a doctor,
Both to adore her and instruct her;
I'll give her what she most admires,   500
Among those venerable sires.
Cadenus is a subject fit,
Grown old in politics and wit,
Caressed by ministers of state,
Of half mankind the dread and hate.
Whate'er vexations love attend,
She need no rivals apprehend.
Her sex, with universal voice,
Must laugh at her capricious choice.'

    Cadenus many things had writ: 510
Vanessa much esteemed his wit,
And called for his poetic works;
Meantime the boy in secret lurks,
And while the book was in her hand,
The urchin from his private stand

Took aim, and shot with all his strength
A dart of such prodigious length,
It pierced the feeble volume through,
And deep transfixed her bosom too.
Some lines, more moving than the rest,   520
Stuck to the point that pierced her breast,
And born directly to the heart,
With pains unknown increased her smart.

Vanessa, not in years a score,
Dreams of a gown of forty-four;
Imaginary charms can find,
In eyes with reading almost blind:
Cadenus now no more appears
Declined in health, advanced in years.
She fancies music in his tongue,   530
Nor further looks, but thinks him young.
What mariner is not afraid,
To venture in a ship decayed?
What planter will attempt to yoke
A sapling with a falling oak?
As years increase, she brighter shines,
Cadenus with each day declines,
And he must fall a prey to time,
While she continues in her prime.

Cadenus, common forms apart,   540
In every scene had kept his heart;
Had sighed and languished, vowed and writ,
For pastime, or to show his wit;
But time, and books, and state affairs,
Had spoiled his fashionable airs;
He now could praise, esteem, approve,
But understood not what was love.
His conduct might have made him styled
A father, and the nymph his child.
That innocent delight he took   550
To see the virgin mind her book,
Was but the master's secret joy

In school to hear the finest boy.
Her knowledge with her fancy grew;
She hourly pressed for something new;
Ideas came into her mind
So fast, his lessons lagged behind;
She reasoned, without plodding long,
Nor ever gave her judgement wrong. 560
But now a sudden change was wrought;
She minds no longer what he taught.
She wished her tutor were her lover;
Resolved she would her flame discover:
And when Cadenus would expound
Some notion subtle or profound,
The nymph would gently press his hand,
As if she seemed to understand;
Or dextrously dissembling chance,
Would sigh, and steal a secret glance.
Cadenus was amazed to find 570
Such marks of a distracted mind;
For though she seemed to listen more
To all he spoke, than e'er before,
He found her thoughts would absent range,
Yet guessed not whence could spring the change.
And first he modestly conjectures
His pupil might be tired with lectures;
Which helped to mortify his pride,
Yet gave him not the heart to chide:
But, in a mild dejected strain, 580
At last he ventured to complain:
Said, she should be no longer teased;
Might have her freedom when she pleased;
Was now convinced he acted wrong,
To hide her from the world so long,
And in dull studies to engage
One of her tender sex and age;
That every nymph with envy owned,
How she might shine in the *grand monde*,
And every shepherd was undone 590
To see her cloistered like a nun.

This was a visionary scheme:
He waked, and found it but a dream;
A project far above his skill,
For nature must be nature still.
If he was bolder than became
A scholar to a courtly dame,
She might excuse a man of letters;
Thus tutors often treat their betters.
And since his talk offensive grew,   600
He came to take his last adieu.

Vanessa, filled with just disdain,
Would still her dignity maintain,
Instructed from her early years
To scorn the art of female tears.

Had he employed his time so long,
To teach her what was right or wrong,
Yet could such notions entertain,
That all his lectures were in vain?
She owned the wandering of her thoughts,   610
But he must answer for her faults.
She well remembered to her cost,
That all his lessons were not lost.
Two maxims she could still produce,
And sad experience taught their use:
That virtue, pleased by being shown,
Knows nothing which it dare not own;
Can make us without fear disclose
Our inmost secrets to our foes;
That common forms were not designed   620
Directors to a noble mind.
'Now,' said the nymph, 'to let you see
My actions with your rules agree,
That I can vulgar forms despise,
And have no secrets to disguise;
I knew by what you said and writ,
How dangerous things were men of wit;
You cautioned me against their charms,

But never gave me equal arms;
Your lessons found the weakest part,   630
Aimed at the head, but reached the heart.'

    Cadenus felt within him rise
Shame, disappointment, guilt, surprise.
He knew not how to reconcile
Such language with her usual style:
And yet her words were so expressed
He could not hope she spoke in jest.
His thoughts had wholly been confined
To form and cultivate her mind.
He hardly knew, till he was told,
Whether the nymph were young or old;   640
Had met her in a public place,
Without distinguishing her face;
Much less could his declining age
Vanessa's earliest thoughts engage;
And if her youth indifference met,
His person must contempt beget;
Or grant her passion be sincere,
How shall his innocence be clear?
Appearances were all so strong,   650
The world must think him in the wrong;
Would say, he made a treacherous use
Of wit, to flatter and seduce;
The town would swear he had betrayed,
By magic spells, the harmless maid;
And every beau would have his jokes,
That scholars were like other folks;
And when Platonic flights were over,
The tutor turned a mortal lover!
So tender of the young and fair!   660
It showed a true paternal care –
'Five thousand guineas in her purse!
The doctor might have fancied worse . . .'

    Hardly at length he silence broke,
And faltered every word he spoke;

Interpreting her complaisance,
Just as a man *sans consequence*.
She rallied well, he always knew:
Her manner now was something new;
And what she spoke was in an air,   670
As serious as a tragic player.
But those who aim at ridicule
Should fix upon some certain rule,
Which fairly hints they are in jest,
Else he must enter his protest:
For let a man be ne'er so wise,
He may be caught with sober lies;
A science which he never taught,
And, to be free, was dearly bought;
For, take it in its proper light,   680
'Tis just what coxcombs call a 'bite'.

But not to dwell on things minute,
Vanessa finished the dispute,
Brought weighty arguments to prove
That reason was her guide in love.
She thought he had himself described,
His doctrines when she first imbibed;
What he had planted, now was grown;
His virtues she might call her own;
As he approves, as he dislikes,   690
Love or contempt, her fancy strikes.
Self-love, in nature rooted fast,
Attends us first, and leaves us last:
Why she likes him, admire not at her;
She loves herself, and that's the matter.
How was her tutor wont to praise
The geniuses of ancient days!
(Those authors he so oft had named,
For learning, wit, and wisdom famed);
Was struck with love, esteem, and awe,   700
For persons whom he never saw.
Suppose Cadenus flourished then,
He must adore such godlike men.

If one short volume could comprise
All that was witty, learned, and wise,
How would it be esteemed, and read,
Although the writer long were dead!
If such an author were alive,
How would all for his friendship strive,
And come in crowds to see his face!   710
And this she takes to be her case.
Cadenus answers every end,
The book, the author, and the friend.
The utmost her desires will reach,
Is but to learn what he can teach:
His converse is a system, fit
Alone to fill up all her wit;
While every passion of her mind
In him is centred and confined.

    Love can with speech inspire a mute,   720
And taught Vanessa to dispute.
This topic, never touched before,
Displayed her eloquence the more:
Her knowledge, with such pains acquired,
By this new passion grew inspired:
Through this she made all objects pass,
Which gave a tincture o'er the mass:
As rivers, though they bend and twine,
Still to the sea their course incline:
Or, as philosophers, who find   730
Some favourite system to their mind,
In every point to make it fit,
Will force all nature to submit.

    Cadenus, who could ne'er suspect
His lessons would have such effect,
Or be so artfully applied,
Insensibly came on her side.
It was an unforeseen event;
Things took a turn he never meant.
Whoe'er excels in what we prize,   740
Appears a hero to our eyes;

Each girl, when pleased with what is taught,
Will have the teacher in her thought.
When Miss delights in her spinnet,
A fiddler may a fortune get;
A blockhead, with melodious voice
In boarding schools can have his choice;
And oft the dancing-master's art
Climbs from the toe to touch the heart.
In learning let a nymph delight,   750
The pedant gets a mistress by't.
Cadenus, to his grief and shame,
Could scarce oppose Vanessa's flame;
And, though her arguments were strong,
At least could hardly wish them wrong.
Howe'er it came, he could not tell,
But sure she never talked so well.
His pride began to interpose,
Preferred before a crowd of beaux!
So bright a nymph to come unsought,   760
Such wonder by his merit wrought:
'Tis merit must with her prevail,
He never knew her judgement fail;
She noted all she ever read,
And had a most discerning head.

'Tis an old maxim in the schools,
That vanity's the food of fools;
Yet now and then your men of wit
Will condescend to take a bit.
So when Cadenus could not hide,   770
He chose to justify his pride;
Construing the passion she had shown,
Much to her praise, more to his own.
Nature in him had merit placed,
In her, a most judicious taste.
Love, hitherto a transient guest,
Ne'er held possession of his breast;
So long attending at the gate,
Disdained to enter in so late.

Love, why do we one passion call,   780
When 'tis a compound of them all?
Where hot and cold, where sharp and sweet,
In all their equipages meet;
Where pleasures mixed with pains appear,
Sorrow with joy, and hope with fear;
Wherein his dignity and age
Forbid Cadenus to engage.
But friendship in its greatest height,
A constant, rational delight,
On virtue's basis fixed to last,   790
When love's allurements long are past,
Which gently warms, but cannot burn,
He gladly offers in return:
His want of passion will redeem,
With gratitude, respect, esteem:
With that devotion we bestow,
When goddesses appear below.

   While thus Cadenus entertains
Vanessa in exalted strains,
The nymph in sober words entreats   800
A truce with all sublime conceits.
For why such raptures, flights, and fancies,
To her, who durst not read romances?
In lofty style to make replies,
Which he had taught her to despise?
But when her tutor will affect
Devotion, duty, and respect,
He fairly abdicates his throne:
The government is now her own;
He has a forfeiture incurred;   810
She vows to take him at his word,
And hopes he will not think it strange,
If both should now their stations change.
The nymph will have her turn, to be
The tutor; and the pupil, he:
Though she already can discern,
Her scholar is not apt to learn;

Or wants capacity to reach
The science she designs to teach:
Wherein his genius was below   820
The skill of every common beau,
Who, though he cannot spell, is wise
Enough to read a lady's eyes,
And will each accidental glance
Interpret for a kind advance.

But what success Vanessa met,
Is to the world a secret yet:
Whether the nymph, to please her swain,
Talks in a high romantic strain;
Or whether he at last descends   830
To act with less seraphic ends;
Or, to compound the business, whether
They temper love and books together;
Must never to mankind be told,
Nor shall the conscious Muse unfold.

Meantime the mournful Queen of Love
Led but a weary life above.
She ventures now to leave the skies,
Grown by Vanessa's conduct wise:
For though by one perverse event   840
Pallas had crossed her first intent;
Though her design was not obtained,
Yet had she much experience gained;
And, by the project vainly tried,
Could better now the cause decide.

She gave due notice, that both parties,
Coram Regina prox' die Martis,
Should at their peril, without fail,
Come and appear, and save their bail.
All met, and silence thrice proclaimed   850
One lawyer to each side was named.
The judge discovered in her face
Resentments for her late disgrace;

And, full of anger, shame and grief,
Directed them to mind their brief;
Nor spend their time to show their reading;
She'd have a summary proceeding.
She gathered, under every head,
The sum of what each lawyer said;
Gave her own reasons last, and then   860
Decreed the cause against the men.

But in a weighty cause like this,
To show she did not judge amiss,
Which evil tongues might else report,
She made a speech in open court;
Wherein she grievously complains,
How she was cheated by the swains;
On whose petition (humbly showing
That women were not worth the wooing;
And that unless the sex would mend,   870
The race of lovers soon must end)
She was at Lord knows what expense
To form a nymph of wit and sense;
A model for her sex designed,
Who never could one lover find.
She saw her favour was misplaced;
The fellows had a wretched taste;
She needs must tell them to their face,
They were a stupid, senseless race:
And were she to begin again,   880
She'd study to reform the men;
Or add some grain of folly more
To women than they had before,
To put them on an equal foot;
And this, or nothing else, would do't.
This might their mutual fancy strike,
Since every being loves its like.

But now, repenting what was done,
She left all business to her son:
She puts the world in his possession,   890
And let him use it at discretion.

The crier was ordered to dismiss
The court, so made his last 'Oyez!'
The goddess would no longer wait;
But, rising from her chair of state,
Left all below at six and seven,
Harnessed her doves, and flew to heaven.

The Fable of Midas

Midas, we are in story told,
Turned everything he touched to gold:
He chipped his bread; the pieces round
Glittered like spangles on the ground:
A codling, e'er it went his lip in,
Would straight become a golden pippin:
He called for drink, you saw him sup
Potable gold in golden cup.
His empty paunch that he might fill,
He sucked his victuals through a quill;   10
Untouched it passed between his grinders,
Or't had been happy for gold-finders.
He cocked his hat, you would have said
Mambrino's helm adorned his head.
Whene'er he chanced his hands to lay,
On magazines of corn or hay,
Gold ready coined appeared, instead
Of paltry provender and bread:
Hence we are by wise farmers told,
Old hay is equal to old gold;   20
And hence a critic deep maintains,
We learned to weigh our gold by grains.

This fool had got a lucky hit,
And people fancied he had wit:

Two gods their skill in music tried,
And both chose Midas to decide;
He against Phoebus' harp decreed,
And gave it for Pan's oaten reed:
The god of wit to show his grudge,
Clapped asses' ears upon the judge, 30
A goodly pair, erect and wide,
Which he could neither gild nor hide.

And now the virtue of his hands,
Was lost among Pactolus sands,
Against whose torrent while he swims,
The golden scurf peels off his limbs:
Fame spreads the news, and people travel
From far, to gather golden gravel;
Midas, exposed to all their jeers,
Had lost his art, and kept his ears. 40

This tale inclines the gentle reader,
To think upon a certain leader,
To whom from Midas down, descends
That virtue in the fingers' ends.
What else by perquisites are meant,
By pensions, bribes, and three per cent?
By places and commissions sold,
And turning dung itself to gold?
By starving in the midst of store,
As t'other Midas did before? 50

None e'er did modern Midas choose,
Subject or patron of his Muse,
But found him thus their merit scan,
That Phoebus must give place to Pan:
He values not the poet's praise,
Nor will exchange his plums for bays:
To Pan alone, rich misers call,
And there's the jest, for Pan is *all*:
Here English wits will be to seek,
Howe'er, 'tis all one in the Greek. 60

Besides, it plainly now appears,
Our Midas, too, has asses' ears;
Where every fool his mouth applies,
And whispers in a thousand lies;
Such gross delusions could not pass,
Through any ears but of an ass.

But gold defiles with frequent touch,
There's nothing fouls the hands so much:
And scholars give it for the cause,
Of British Midas' dirty paws;   70
Which while the senate strove to scour,
They washed away the chemic power.
While he his utmost strength applied,
To swim against this popular tide,
The golden spoils flew off apace;
Here fell a pension, there a place:
The torrent, merciless, imbibes
Commissions, perquisites, and bribes;
By their own weight sunk to the bottom;
Much good may do 'em that have caught 'em.   80
And Midas now neglected stands,
With asses' ears, and dirty hands.

A Satirical Elegy on the Death of a Late Famous General

His Grace! impossible! what, dead!
Of old age too, and in his bed!
And could that Mighty Warrior fall?
And so inglorious, after all!
Well, since he's gone, no matter how,
The last loud trump must wake him now;
And, trust me, as the noise grows stronger,
He'd wish to sleep a little longer.

And could he be indeed so old
As by the newspapers we're told?   10
Threescore, I think, is pretty high;
'Twas time in conscience he should die!
This world he cumbered long enough;
He burnt his candle to the snuff;
And that's the reason, some folks think,
He left behind *so great a stink*.
Behold his funeral appears,
Nor widow's sighs, nor orphan's tears,
Wont at such times each heart to pierce,
Attend the progress of his hearse.   20
But what of that? his friends may say,
He had those honours in his day.
True to his profit and his pride,
He made them weep before he died.

  Come hither, all ye empty things!
Ye bubbles raised by breath of kings!
Who float upon the tide of state,
Come hither, and behold your fate!
Let Pride be taught by this rebuke,
How very mean a thing's a Duke;   30
From all his ill-got honours flung,
Turned to that dirt from whence he sprung.

The Furniture of a Woman's Mind

A set of phrases learned by rote;
A passion for a scarlet coat;
When at a play to laugh, or cry,
But cannot tell the reason why:
Never to hold her tongue a minute,
While all she prates has nothing in it.
Whole hours can with a coxcomb sit,
And take his nonsense all for wit:

Her learning mounts to read a song,
But half the words pronouncing wrong;   10
Has every repartee in store,
She spoke ten thousand times before.
Can ready compliments supply
On all occasions, cut and dry;
Such hatred to a parson's gown,
The sight will put her in a swoon;
For conversation well endued,
She calls it witty to be rude;
And, placing raillery in railing,
Will tell aloud your greatest failing;   20
Nor makes a scruple to expose
Your bandy leg, or crooked nose;
Can, at her morning tea, run o'er
The scandal of the day before;
Improving hourly in her skill,
To cheat and wrangle at quadrille.

    In choosing lace, a critic nice,
Knows to a groat the lowest price;
Can in her female clubs dispute,
What lining best the silk will suit;   30
What colours each complexion match,
And where with art to place a patch.
If chance a mouse creeps in her sight,
Can finely counterfeit a fright;
So sweetly screams, if it comes near her,
She ravishes all hearts to hear her.
Can dexterously her husband tease,
By taking fits whene'er she please;
By frequent practice learns the trick
At proper seasons to be sick;   40
Thinks nothing gives one airs so pretty,
At once creating love and pity.
If Molly happens to be careless,
And but neglects to warm her hair-lace,
She gets a cold as sure as death,
And vows she scarce can fetch her breath;

Admires how modest women can
Be so *robustious* like a man.

In party, furious to her power;
A bitter Whig, or Tory sour;   50
Her arguments directly tend
Against the side she would defend;
Will prove herself a Tory plain,
From principles the Whigs maintain;
And, to defend the Whiggish cause,
Her topics from the Tories draws.

O yes! If any man can find
More virtues in a woman's mind,
Let them be sent to Mrs Harding;
She'll pay the charges to a farthing: 60
Take notice, she has my commission
To add them in the next edition;
They may outsell a better thing;
So halloo boys! God save the King.

The Progress of Beauty

When first Diana leaves her bed,
Vapours and steams her looks disgrace,
A frowzy dirty coloured red
Sits on her cloudy wrinkled face.

But by degrees, when mounted high,
Her artificial face appears
Down from her window in the sky,
Her spots are gone, her visage clears.

'Twixt earthly females and the moon,
All parallels exactly run: 10

If Celia should appear too soon,
Alas, the nymph would be undone!

To see her from her pillow rise
All reeking in a cloudy steam,
Cracked lips, foul teeth, and gummy eyes;
Poor Strephon, how would he blaspheme!

The soot, or powder which was wont
To make her hair look black as jet,
Falls from her tresses on her front
A mingled mass of dirt and sweat.   20

Three colours, black, and red, and white,
So graceful in their proper place,
Remove them to a different site,
They form a frightful hideous face.

For instance, when the lily skips
Into the precincts of the rose,
And takes possession of the lips,
Leaving the purple to the nose.

So Celia went entire to bed,
All her complexions safe and sound;   30
But when she rose, white, black, and red,
Though still in sight, had changed their ground.

The black, which would not be confined,
A more inferior station seeks,
Leaving the fiery red behind,
And mingles in her muddy cheeks.

The paint by perspiration cracks,
And falls in rivulets of sweat,
On either side you see the tracks,
While at her chin the confluents met.   40

A skilful housewife thus her thumb
With spittle while she spins, anoints,

And thus the brown meanders come
In trickling streams betwixt her joints.

But Celia can with ease reduce,
By help of pencil, paint and brush,
Each colour to its place and use,
And teach her cheeks again to blush.

She knows her early self no more,
But filled with admiration stands,   50
As other painters oft adore
The workmanship of their own hands.

Thus, after four important hours,
Celia's the wonder of her sex;
Say, which among the heavenly powers
Could cause such marvellous effects?

Venus, indulgent to her kind,
Gave women all their hearts could wish,
When first she taught them where to find
White lead and Lusitanian dish.   60

Love with white lead cements his wings;
White lead was sent us to repair
Two brightest, brittlest, earthly things,
A lady's face, and china-ware.

She ventures now to lift the sash,
The window is her proper sphere;
Ah, lovely nymph! be not too rash,
Nor let the beaux approach too near.

Take pattern by your sister star,
Delude at once, and bless our sight,   70
When you are seen, be seen from far,
And chiefly choose to shine by night.

In the Pall Mall when passing by,
Keep up the glasses of your chair,

Then each transported fop will cry,
'God damn me Jack, she's wondrous fair.'

But art no longer can prevail,
When the materials all are gone,
The best mechanic hand must fail,
When nothing's left to work upon.   80

Matter, as wise logicians say,
Cannot without a form subsist;
And form, say I, as well as they,
Must fail, if matter brings no grist.

And this is fair Diana's case;
For all astrologers maintain,
Each night a bit drops off her face,
While mortals say she's in her wane.

While Partridge wisely shows the cause
Efficient of the moon's decay,   90
That Cancer with his poisonous claws,
Attacks her in the Milky Way:

But Gadbury, in art profound,
From her pale cheeks pretends to show,
That swain Endymion is not sound,
Or else, that Mercury's her foe.

But let the cause be what it will,
In half a month she looks so thin,
That Flamsteed can, with all his skill,
See but her forehead and her chin.   100

Yet, as she wastes, she grows discreet,
Till midnight never shows her head:
So rotting Celia strolls the street,
When sober folks are all abed.

For sure if this be Luna's fate,
Poor Celia, but of mortal race,

In vain expects a longer date
To the materials of her face.

When Mercury her tresses mows,
To think of black-lead combs is vain,   110
No painting can restore a nose,
Nor will her teeth return again.

Two balls of glass may serve for eyes,
White lead can plaster up a cleft,
But these alas, are poor supplies
If neither cheeks, nor lips be left.

Ye powers, who over love preside,
Since mortal beauties drop so soon,
If you would have us well supplied,
Send us new nymphs with each new moon.   120

The Progress of Marriage

Aetatis suae fifty-two,
A rich divine began to woo
A handsome, young, imperious girl,
Nearly related to an Earl.
Her parents and her friends consent,
The couple to the temple went:
They first invite the Cyprian Queen,
'Twas answered, she would not be seen.
The Graces next, and all the Muses
Were bid in form, but sent excuses.   10
Juno attended at the porch
With farthing candle for a torch,
While Mistress Iris held her train,

The faded bow distilling rain.
Then Hebe came and took her place,
But showed no more than half her face.

Whate'er these dire forebodings meant,
In mirth the wedding-day was spent.
The wedding-day, you take me right,
I promise nothing for the night,   20
The bridegroom, dressed to make a figure,
Assumes an artificial vigour;
A flourished nightcap on, to grace
His ruddy, wrinkled, smirking face,
Like the faint red upon a pippin,
Half withered by a winter's keeping.

And, thus set out this happy pair,
The swain is rich, the nymph is fair;
But, what I gladly would forget,
The swain is old, the nymph coquette.   30
Both from the goal together start;
Scarce run a step before they part;
No common ligament that binds
The various textures of their minds,
Their thoughts, and actions, hopes, and fears,
Less corresponding than their years.
Her spouse desires his coffee soon,
She rises to her tea at noon.
While he goes out to cheapen books,
She at the glass consults her looks;   40
While Betty's buzzing at her ear,
Lord, what a dress these parsons wear!
So odd a choice, how could she make!
Wished him a colonel for her sake,
Then on her fingers' ends she counts
Exact to what his age amounts,
The Dean, she heard her uncle say,
Is sixty, if he be a day;
His ruddy cheeks are no diguise;
You see the crow's feet round his eyes.   50

At one she rambles to the shops,
To cheapen tea, and talk with fops;
Or calls a council of her maids
And tradesmen, to compare brocades.
Her weighty morning business o'er,
Sits down to dinner just at four;
Minds nothing that is done or said,
Her evening work so fills her head.
The Dean, who used to dine at one,
Is mawkish, and his stomach gone;   60
In threadbare gown, would scarce a louse hold,
Looks like the chaplain of the household;
Beholds her from the chaplain's place
In French brocades and Flanders lace;
He wonders what employs her brain,
But never asks, or asks in vain;
His mind is full of other cares,
And in the sneaking parson's airs
Computes, that half a parish dues
Will hardly find his wife in shoes.   70

Canst thou imagine, dull divine,
'Twill gain her love, to make her fine?
Hath she no other wants beside?
You raise desire as well as pride,
Enticing coxcombs to adore,
And teach her to despise thee more.

If in her coach she'll condescend
To place him at the hinder end,
Her hoop is hoist above his nose,
His odious gown would soil her clothes,   80
And drops him at the church, to pray,
While she drives on to see the play.
He, like an orderly divine,
Comes home a quarter after nine,
And meets her hasting to the ball:
Her chairmen push him from the wall.
He enters in, and walks upstairs,
And calls the family to prayers,

Then goes alone to take his rest
In bed, where he can spare her best.   90
At five the footmen make a din,
Her ladyship is just come in;
The masquerade began at two,
She stole away with much ado,
And shall be chid this afternoon
For leaving company so soon:
She'll say, and she may truly say't,
She can't abide to stay out late.

But now, though scarce a twelve month married,
Poor Lady Jane has thrice miscarried,   100
The cause, alas, is quickly guessed,
The town has whispered round the jest:
Think on some remedy in time,
You find his Reverence past his prime,
Already dwindled to a lathe:
No other way but try the Bath.

For Venus, rising from the ocean,
Infused a strong prolific potion,
That mixed with Achelous' spring,
The 'hornéd flood', as poets sing: 110
Who with an English beauty smitten
Ran underground from Greece to Britain;
The genial virtue with him brought,
And gave the nymph a plenteous draught;
Then fled, and left his horn behind,
For husbands past their youth to find;
The nymph, who still with passion burned,
Was to a boiling fountain turned,
Where childless wives crowd every morn
To drink in Achelous' horn.   120
And here the father often gains
That title by another's pains.

Hither, though much against his grain,
The Dean has carried Lady Jane.

He for a while would not consent,
But vowed his money all was spent:
His money spent! a clownish reason!
And must my Lady slip her season?
The doctor, with a double fee,
Was bribed to make the Dean agree.   130

Here, all diversions of the place
Are proper in my Lady's case:
With which she patiently complies,
Merely because her friends advise;
His money and her time employs
In music, raffling-rooms, and toys;
Or in the Cross Bath, seeks an heir
Since others oft have found one there;
Where if the Dean by chance appears
It shames his cassock and his years.   140
He keeps his distance in the gallery
Till banished by some coxcomb's raillery;
For, it would his character expose
To bathe among the belles and beaux.

So have I seen, within a pen,
Young ducklings, fostered by a hen;
But when let out, they run and muddle
As instinct leads them, in a puddle;
The sober hen, not born to swim
With mournful note clucks round the brim.   150

The Dean, with all his best endeavour,
Gets not an heir, but gets a fever;
A victim to the last essays
Of vigour in declining days.
He dies, and leaves his mourning mate
(What could he less?) his whole estate.

The widow goes through all the forms:
New lovers now will come in swarms.
Oh, may I see her soon dispensing

Her favours to some broken ensign!   160
Him let her marry, for his face,
And only coat of tarnished lace;
To turn her naked out of doors,
And spend her jointure on his whores:
But, for a parting present, leave her
A rooted pox to last forever!

Strephon and Chloe

Of Chloe all the town has rung,
By every size of poet sung:
So beautiful a nymph appears
But once in twenty thousand years:
By Nature formed with nicest care,
And faultless to a single hair.
Her graceful mien, her shape, and face,
Confessed her of no mortal race:
And then, so nice, and so genteel;
Such cleanliness from head to heel: 10
No humours gross, or frowzy steams,
No noisome whiffs, or sweaty streams,
Before, behind, above, below,
Could from her taintless body flow:
Would so discreetly things dispose,
None ever saw her pluck a rose.
Her dearest comrades never caught her
Squat on her hams, to make maid's water.
You'd swear that so divine a creature
Felt no necessities of nature.   20
In summer had she walked the town,
Her armpits would not stain her gown:
At country dances, not a nose
Could in the dog-days smell her toes.
Her milk-white hands, both palms and backs,
Like ivory dry, and soft as wax.

Her hands, the softest ever felt,
Though cold would burn, though dry would melt.

Dear Venus, hide this wondrous maid,
Nor let her loose to spoil your trade.　　　　30
While she engrosseth every swain,
You but o'er half the world can reign.
Think what a case all men are now in,
What ogling, sighing, toasting, vowing!
What powdered wigs! What flames and darts!
What hampers full of bleeding hearts!
What sword-knots! What poetic strains!
What billet-doux, and clouded canes!

But Strephon sighed so loud and strong,
He blew a settlement along;　　　　40
And bravely drove his rivals down,
With coach and six, and house in town.
The bashful nymph no more withstands,
Because her dear papa commands.
The charming couple now unites;
Proceed we to the marriage rites.

Imprimis, at the temple porch
Stood Hymen with a flaming torch.
The smiling Cyprian goddess brings
Her infant loves with purple wings;　　　　50
And pigeons billing, sparrows treading,
Fair emblems of a fruitful wedding.
The Muses next in order follow,
Conducted by their squire, Apollo:
Then Mercury with silver tongue,
And Hebe, goddess ever young.
Behold the bridegroom and his bride,
Walk hand in hand, and side by side;
She, by the tender Graces dressed,
But he, by Mars, in scarlet vest.　　　　60
The nymph was covered with her *flammeum*,
And Phoebus sung the epithalamium.
And last, to make the matter sure,

Dame Juno brought a priest demure.
Luna was absent on pretence
Her time was not till nine months hence.

The rites performed, the parson paid,
In state returned the grand parade;
With loud huzza's from all the boys,
That now the pair must *crown their joys*.   70

But still the hardest part remains.
Strephon had long perplexed his brains,
How with so high a nymph he might
Demean himself the wedding-night:
For, as he viewed his person round,
Mere mortal flesh was all he found:
His hand, his neck, his mouth, and feet
Were duly washed to keep 'em sweet;
(With other parts that shall be nameless,
The ladies else might think me shameless.)   80
The weather and his love were hot;
And should he struggle; I know what –
Why let it go, if I must tell it –
He'll sweat, and then the nymph will smell it.
While she a goddess dyed in grain
Was unsusceptible of stain:
And, Venus-like, her fragrant skin
Exhaled ambrosia from within:
Can such a deity endure
A mortal human touch impure?   90
How did the humbled swain detest
His prickled beard, and hairy breast!
His nightcap, bordered round with lace,
Could give no softness to his face.

Yet, if the goddess could be kind,
What endless raptures must he find!
And goddesses have now and then
Come down to visit mortal men:
To visit and to court them too:
A certain goddess, God knows who,   100

(As in a book he heard it read)
Took Colonel Peleus to her bed.
But, what if he should lose his life
By venturing *on* his heavenly wife?
For Strephon could remember well,
That, once he heard a schoolboy tell,
How Semele, of mortal race,
By thunder died in Jove's embrace;
And what if daring Strephon dies
By lightning shot from Chloe's eyes?   110

    While these reflections filled his head,
The bride was put in form to bed:
He followed, stripped, and in he crept,
But, awfully his distance kept.

    Now, ponder well, ye parents dear;
Forbid your daughters guzzling beer;
And make them every afternoon
Forbear their tea, or drink it soon;
That, e'er to bed they venture up,
They may discharge it every sup;   120
If not, they must in evil plight
Be often forced to rise at night.
Keep them to wholesome food confined,
Nor let them taste what causes wind:
('Tis this the sage of Samos means,
Forbidding his disciples beans)
O, think what evils must ensue;
Miss Moll, the jade, will burn it blue:
And when she once has got the art,
She cannot help it for her heart;   130
But out it flies, even when she meets
Her bridegroom in the wedding-sheets.
Carminative and diuretic,
Will damp all passions sympathetic;
And love such niceties requires,
One blast will put out all his fires.
Since husbands get behind the scene,
The wife should study to be clean;

Nor give the smallest room to guess
The time when wants of nature press;   140
But, after marriage, practise more
Decorum than she did before;
To keep her spouse deluded still,
And make him fancy what she will.

In bed we left the married pair;
'Tis time to show how things went there.
Strephon, who had been often told,
That fortune still assists the bold,
Resolved to make his first attack:
But Chloe drove him fiercely back.   150
How could a nymph so chaste as Chloe,
With constitution cold and snowy,
Permit a brutish man to touch her?
Even lambs by instinct fly the butcher.
Resistance on the wedding night
Is what our maidens claim by right:
And Chloe, 'tis by all agreed,
Was maid in thought, and word, and deed.
Yet some assign a different reason;
That Strephon chose no proper season.   160

Say, fair ones, must I make a pause,
Or freely tell the secret cause?

Twelve cups of tea, (with grief I speak)
Had now constrained the nymph to leak.
This point must needs be settled first:
The bride must either void or burst.
Then, see the dire effect of pease,
Think what can give the colic ease.
The nymph oppressed before, behind,
As ships are tossed by waves and wind,   170
Steals out her hand, by nature led,
And brings a vessel into bed:
Fair utensil, as smooth and white
As Chloe's skin, almost as bright.

Strephon who heard the foaming rill
As from a mossy cliff distil,
Cried out, 'Ye gods! what sound is this?
Can Chloe, heavenly Chloe piss?'
But when he smelt a noisome steam
Which oft attends that lukewarm stream;   180
(Salerno both together joins
As sovereign medicines for the loins)
And, though contrived, we may suppose
To slip his ears, yet struck his nose:
He found her, while the scent increased,
As *mortal* as himself at least.
But, soon with like occasions pressed,
He boldly sent his hand in quest,
(Inspired with courage from his bride,)
To reach the pot on t'other side.   190
And as he filled the reeking vase,
Let fly a rouser in her face.

The little Cupids hovering round,
(As pictures prove) with garlands crowned,
Abashed at what they saw and heard,
Flew off, nor ever more appeared.

Adieu to ravishing delights,
High raptures, and romantic flights;
To goddesses so heavenly sweet,
Expiring shepherds at their feet;   200
To silver meads, and shady bowers,
Dressed up with amaranthine flowers.

How great a change! how quickly made!
They learn to call a spade, a spade.
They soon from all constraints are freed;
Can see each other do their need.
On box of cedar sits the wife,
And makes it warm for 'dearest life'.
And, by the beastly way of thinking,
Find great society in stinking.   210
Now Strephon daily entertains

His Chloe in the homeliest strains;
And Chloe, more experienced grown,
With interest pays him back his own.
No maid at court is less ashamed,
Howe'er for selling bargains famed,
Than she, to name her parts behind,
Or when abed, to let out wind.

    Fair Decency, celestial maid!
Descend from Heaven to Beauty's aid;   220
Though Beauty must beget Desire,
'Tis thou must fan the Lover's fire;
For Beauty, like supreme Dominion,
Is best supported by Opinion:
If Decency brings no supplies,
Opinion falls, and Beauty dies.

    To see some radiant nymph appear
In all her glittering birthday gear,
You think some goddess from the sky
Descended, ready cut and dry: 230
But, e'er you sell yourself to laughter,
Consider well what may come after;
For fine ideas vanish fast,
While all the gross and filthy last.

    O Strephon, e'er that fatal day
When Chloe stole your heart away,
Had you but through a cranny spied
On house of ease your future bride,
In all the postures of her face,
Which nature gives in such a case;   240
Distortions, groanings, strainings, heavings;
'Twere better you had licked her leavings,
Than from experience find too late
Your goddess grown a filthy mate.
Your fancy then had always dwelt
On what you saw, and what you smelt;
Would still the same ideas give ye,
As when you spied her on the privy;

And, spite of Chloe's charms divine,
Your heart had been as whole as mine.   250

    Authorities, both old and recent,
Direct that women must be decent;
And, from the spouse each blemish hide,
More than from all the world beside.

    Unjustly all our nymphs complain,
Their empire holds so short a reign;
Is, after marriage, lost so soon,
It hardly holds the honeymoon:
For, if they keep not what they caught,
It is entirely their own fault.   260
They take possession of the crown,
And then throw all their weapons down;
Though by the politicians' scheme
Whoe'er arrives at power supreme,
Those arts by which at first they gain it,
They still must practise to attain it.

    What various ways our females take,
To pass for wits before a rake!
And in the fruitless search pursue
All other methods but the true!   270

    Some try to learn polite behaviour,
By reading books against their Saviour;
Some call it witty to reflect
On every natural defect;
Some show they never want explaining,
To comprehend a double meaning.
But, sure a tell-tale out of school
Is, of all wits, the greatest fool;
Whose rank imaginations fills
Her heart, and from her lips distils;   280
You'd think she uttered from behind,
Or at her mouth was breaking wind.

    Why is a handsome wife adored
By every coxcomb, but her lord?

From yonder puppet-man inquire,
Who wisely hides his wood and wire:
Show Sheba's queen completely dressed,
And Solomon in royal vest:
But, view them littered on the floor,
Or strung on pegs behind the door;   290
Punch is exactly of a piece
With Lorraine's Duke, and Prince of Greece.

    A prudent builder should forecast
How long the stuff is like to last;
And, carefully observe the ground,
To build on some foundation sound.
What house, when its materials crumble,
Must not inevitably tumble?
What edifice can long endure,
Raised on a basis unsecure?   300
Rash mortals, e'er you take a wife,
Contrive your pile to last for life;
Since beauty scarce endures a day,
And youth so swiftly glides away;
Why will you make yourself a bubble
To build on sand with hay and stubble?

    On sense and wit your passion found,
By decency cemented round;
Let prudence with good nature strive,
To keep esteem and love alive.   310
Then come old age whene'er it will,
Your friendship shall continue still:
And thus a mutual gentle fire,
Shall never but with life expire.

A Beautiful Young Nymph Going to Bed

Written for the Honour of the Fair Sex

Corinna, pride of Drury Lane,
For whom no shepherd sighs in vain;
Never did Covent Garden boast
So bright a battered, strolling toast;
No drunken rake to pick her up,
No cellar where on tick to sup;
Returning at the midnight hour,
Four storeys climbing to her bower;
Then, seated on a three-legged chair,
Takes off her artificial hair;   10
Now picking out a crystal eye,
She wipes it clean, and lays it by.
Her eyebrows from a mouse's hide,
Stuck on with art on either side,
Pulls off with care, and first displays 'em,
Then in a play-book smoothly lays 'em.
Now dexterously her plumpers draws,
That serve to fill her hollow jaws.
Untwists a wire; and from her gums
A set of teeth completely comes.   20
Pulls out the rags contrived to prop
Her flabby dugs, and down they drop.
Proceeding on, the lovely goddess
Unlaces next her steel-ribbed bodice,
Which by the operator's skill,
Press down the lumps, the hollows fill.
Up goes her hand, and off she slips
The bolsters that supply her hips.
With gentlest touch, she next explores
Her shankers, issues, running sores;   30
Effects of many a sad disaster,
And then to each applies a plaster:
But must, before she goes to bed,
Rub off the daubs of white and red.
And smooth the furrows in her front,

With greasy paper stuck upon't.
She takes a bolus e'er she sleeps;
And then between two blankets creeps.
With pains of love tormented lies;
Or if she chance to close her eyes,   40
Of Bridewell and the Compter dreams,
And feels the lash, and faintly screams.
Or, by a faithless bully drawn,
At some hedge-tavern lies in pawn;
Or to Jamaica seems transported,
Alone, and by no planter courted;
Or, near Fleet Ditch's oozy brinks,
Surrounded with a hundred stinks,
Belated, seems on watch to lie,
And snap some cully passing by;   50
Or, struck with fear, her fancy runs
On watchmen, constables and duns,
From whom she meets with frequent rubs;
But, never from religious clubs;
Whose favour she is sure to find,
Because she pays them all in kind.

    Corinna wakes. A dreadful sight!
Behold the ruins of the night!
A wicked rat her plaster stole,
Half ate, and dragged it to his hole.   60
The crystal eye, alas, was missed;
And Puss had on her plumpers pissed.
A pigeon picked her issue-peas,
And Shock her tresses filled with fleas.

    The nymph, though in this mangled plight,
Must every morn her limbs unite.
But how shall I describe her arts
To re-collect the scattered parts?
Or show the anguish, toil, and pain,
Of gathering up herself again?   70
The bashful Muse will never bear
In such a scene to interfere.
Corinna in the morning dizened,
Who sees, will spew; who smells, be poisoned.

The Lady's Dressing Room

Five hours, (and who can do it less in?)
By haughty Celia spent in dressing;
The goddess from her chamber issues,
Arrayed in lace, brocade and tissues.
Strephon, who found the room was void,
And Betty otherwise employed,
Stole in, and took a strict survey,
Of all the litter as it lay:
Whereof, to make the matter clear,
An inventory follows here.   10

   And first, a dirty smock appeared,
Beneath the arm-pits well besmeared;
Strephon, the rogue, displayed it wide,
And turned it round on every side.
On such a point, few words are best,
And Strephon bids us guess the rest;
But swears how damnably the men lie,
In calling Celia sweet and cleanly.

   Now listen while he next produces,
The various combs for various uses,   20
Filled up with dirt so closely fixed,
No brush could force a way betwixt;
A paste of composition rare,
Sweat, dandruff, powder, lead and hair;
A forehead cloth with oil upon't
To smooth the wrinkles on her front;
Here alum-flour to stop the steams,
Exhaled from sour unsavoury streams;
There night-gloves made of Tripsy's hide,
Bequeathed by Tripsy when she died;   30
With puppy-water, beauty's help,
Distilled from Tripsy's darling whelp.
Here gallipots and vials placed,
Some filled with washes, some with paste;
Some with pomatum, paints and slops,

And ointments good for scabby chops.
Hard by a filthy basin stands,
Fouled with the scouring of her hands;
The basin takes whatever comes,
The scrapings from her teeth and gums,   40
A nasty compound of all hues,
For here she spits, and here she spews.

But oh! it turned poor Strephon's bowels,
When he beheld and smelt the towels,
Begummed, bemattered, and beslimed,
With dirt, and sweat, and ear-wax grimed;
No object Strephon's eye escapes,
Here, petticoats in frowzy heaps;
Nor be the handkerchiefs forgot,
All varnished o'er with snuff and snot.   50
The stockings why should I expose,
Stained with the marks of stinking toes;
Or greasy coifs and pinners reeking,
Which Celia slept at least a week in?
A pair of tweezers next he found,
To pluck her brows in arches round,
Or hairs that sink the forehead low,
Or on her chin like bristles grow.

The virtues we must not let pass,
Of Celia's magnifying glass;   60
When frighted Strephon cast his eye on't,
It showed the visage of a giant:
A glass that can to sight disclose
The smallest worm in Celia's nose,
And faithfully direct her nail
To squeeze it out from head to tail;
For, catch it nicely by the head,
It must come out alive or dead.

Why, Strephon, will you tell the rest?
And must you needs describe the chest?   70
That careless wench! no creature warn her
To move it out from yonder corner,

But leave it standing full in sight,
For you to exercise your spite!
In vain the workman showed his wit
With rings and hinges counterfeit
To make it seem in this disguise,
A cabinet to vulgar eyes:
Which Strephon ventured to look in,
Resolved to go through thick and thin.   80
He lifts the lid: there needs no more,
He smelt it all the time before.

    As, from within Pandora's box,
When Epimethus oped the locks,
A sudden universal crew
Of human evils upward flew;
He still was comforted to find
That hope at last remained behind.

    So, Strephon, lifting up the lid,
To view what in the chest was hid,   90
The vapours flew from out the vent,
But Strephon, cautious, never meant
The bottom of the pan to grope,
And foul his hands in search of hope.

    O! ne'er may such a vile machine
Be once in Celia's chamber seen!
O! may she better learn to keep
Those 'secrets of the hoary deep.'

    As mutton cutlets, prime of meat,
Which, though with art you salt and beat,   100
As laws of cookery require,
And roast them at the clearest fire;
If from adown the hopeful chops
The fat upon a cinder drops,
To stinking smoke it turns the flame,
Poisoning the flesh from whence it came;
And up exhales a greasy stench,
For which you curse the careless wench:

So things which must not be expressed,
When plumped into the reeking chest,   110
Send up an excremental smell
To taint the parts from which they fell:
The petticoats and gown perfume,
And waft a stink round every room.

Thus finishing his grand survey,
Disgusted Strephon stole away,
Repeating in his amorous fits,
'Oh! Celia, Celia, Celia shits!'

But Vengeance, goddess never sleeping,
Soon punished Strephon for his peeping.   120
His foul imagination links
Each dame he sees with all her stinks:
And, if unsavoury odours fly,
Conceives a lady standing by.
All women his description fits,
And both ideas jump like wits;
By vicious fancy coupled fast,
And still appearing in contrast.

I pity wretched Strephon, blind
To all the charms of womankind.   130
Should I the Queen of Love refuse,
Because she rose from stinking ooze?
To him that looks behind the scene,
Statira's but some pocky quean.

When Celia in her glory shows,
If Strephon would but stop his nose,
(Who now so impiously blasphemes
Her ointments, daubs, and paints, and creams;
Her washes, slops, and every clout,
With which he makes so foul a rout;)   140
He soon would learn to think like me,
And bless his ravished eyes to see
Such order from confusion sprung,
Such gaudy tulips raised from dung.

Cassinus and Peter

A Tragical Elegy

Two college sophs of Cambridge growth,
Both special wits, and lovers both,
Conferring as they used to meet,
On love, and books, in rapture sweet;
(Muse, find me names to fix my metre,
Cassinus this, and t'other Peter)
Friend Peter to Cassinus goes,
To chat a while, and warm his nose:
But such a sight was never seen,
The lad lay swallowed up in spleen.   10
He seemed as just crept out of bed;
One greasy stocking round his head,
The t'other he sat down to darn,
With threads of different coloured yarn.
His breeches torn, exposing wide
A ragged shirt, and tawny hide.
Scorched were his shins, his legs were bare,
But well embrowned with dirt and hair.
A rug was o'er his shoulders thrown;
A rug; for night-gown had he none.   20
His jordan stood in manner fitting
Between his legs, to spew or spit in.
His ancient pipe, in sable dyed,
And half unsmoked, lay by his side.

Him thus accoutred, Peter found,
With eyes in smoke and weeping drowned:
The leavings of his last night's pot
On embers placed, to drink it hot.

'Why, Cassy, thou wilt doze thy pate:
What makes thee lie abed so late?   30
The finch, the linnet, and the thrush,
Their matins chant in every bush:
And I have heard thee oft salute

Aurora with thy early flute.
Heaven send thou hast not got the hyps!
How? not a word come from thy lips?'

Then gave him some familiar thumps,
A college joke to cure the dumps.

The swain at last, with grief oppressed,
Cried, 'Celia!' thrice, and sighed the rest.   40

'Dear Cassy, though to ask I dread,
Yet ask I must. Is Celia dead?'

'How happy I, were that the worst!
But I was fated to be cursed.'

'Come, tell us, has she played the whore?'

'Oh Peter, would it were no more!'

'Why, plague confound her sandy locks!
Say, has the small or greater pox
Sunk down her nose, or seamed her face?
Be easy, 'tis a common case.'   50

'Oh Peter! beauty's but a varnish,
Which time and accidents will tarnish:
But Celia has contrived to blast
Those beauties that might ever last.
Nor can imagination guess,
Nor eloquence divine express,
How that ungrateful charming maid,
My purest passion has betrayed.
Conceive the most envenomed dart,
To pierce an injured lover's heart.'   60

'Why, hang her, though she seemed so coy,
I know she loves the barber's boy.'

'Friend Peter, this I could excuse,
For, every nymph has leave to choose;

Nor, have I reason to complain,
She loves a more deserving swain.
But, oh! how ill thou hast divined
A crime that shocks all humankind;
A deed unknown to female race,
At which the sun should hide his face.   70
Advice in vain you would apply –
Then, leave me to despair and die.
Yet, kind Arcadians, on my urn
These elegies and sonnets burn,
And on the marble grave these rhymes,
A monument to after-times:
"Here Cassy lies, by Celia slain,
And dying, never told his pain."

    'Vain empty world, farewell. But hark,
The loud Cerberian triple bark.   80
And there – behold Alecto stand,
A whip of scorpions in her hand.
Lo, Charon from his leaky wherry,
Beckoning to waft me o'er the ferry.
I come, I come – Medusa, see,
Her serpents hiss direct at me.
Begone; unhand me, hellish fry:
Avaunt – ye cannot say 'twas I.'

    'Dear Cassy, thou must purge and bleed;
I fear thou wilt be mad indeed.   90
But now, by friendship's sacred laws,
I here conjure thee, tell the cause;
And Celia's horrid fact relate;
Thy friend would gladly share thy fate.'

    'To force it out, my heart must rend;
Yet, when conjured by such a friend –
Think, Peter, how my soul is racked!
These eyes, these eyes beheld the fact.
Now, bend thine ear; since out it must:
But, when thou seest me laid in dust,   100
The secret thou shalt ne'er impart;

Not to the nymph that keeps thy heart;
(How would her virgin soul bemoan
A crime to all her sex unknown!)
Nor whisper to the tattling reeds,
The blackest of all female deeds:
Nor blab it on the lonely rocks,
Where Echo sits, and listening, mocks:
Nor let the Zephyr's treacherous gale
Through Cambridge waft the direful tale: 110
Nor to the chattering feathered race,
Discover Celia's foul disgrace.
But, if you fail, my spectre dread,
Attending nightly round your bed:
And yet, I dare confide in you;
So, take my secret, and adieu.

     'Nor, wonder how I lost my wits;
Oh! Celia, Celia, Celia shits!'

Notes

The text follows The Works of J.S., D.D. ed. George Faulkner
(1735), with reference also to The Poems of Jonathan Swift ed. Harold
Williams, 2nd edn (1958) and Jonathan Swift: The Complete Poems
ed. Pat Rogers (1983).

p. 1 *Verses on the Death of Dr Swift, D.S.P.D.*: (written 1731; this
version published by Faulkner, 1739). **Title: D.S.P.D.** Dean of St Patrick's,
Dublin. **1 Rochefoucauld:** (1613–80), French moralist. **47 Pope:**
Alexander (1688–1744), poet and satirist, member of the Scriblerus Club
with Swift, Arbuthnot, Gay, Parnell. **53 Gay:** John (1685–1732), poet
and dramatist, author of *The Beggar's Opera*. **55 Arbuthnot:** John
(1667–1735), writer and physician to Pope. **59 St John:** Henry, first
Viscount Bolingbroke (1678–1751), politician and writer, whose philo-
sophical and political ideas had some influence on the Scriblerians.
59 Pulteney: William (1684–1764), politician, friend of Pope and Gay.
71 proem: introduction. **83 vertigo:** a dizziness, symptom of Swift's
Ménière's disease. **108 Charles the Second:** when Charles II died in
1685, Swift was 18 years old. **117 tropes:** figures of speech. **139 regimen:** diet. **165 Grub-street:** street near Moorfields, London, inhabited
by literary hacks. **168 the Drapier:** Swift's pseudonym for his attack on
Wood's coinage in *The Drapier's Letters*. **179 Lady Suffolk:** Henrietta
Howard (c. 1687–1767), friend to Swift, Pope and Gay. **187 King:**
George II (ruled 1727–60). **189 Chartres:** Francis Charteris
(1675–1732), Scottish landowner, money-lender, gambler, cheat and
rapist, associate of Walpole. **Sir Robert:** Walpole (1676–1745), whig
politician who became first minister of state, and the persistent target of the
Scriblerians' satire. **191 without his shoes:** 'to die in one's shoes' was
criminal argot for being hanged. **194 Will:** see Pulteney, line 59.
196 Bolingbroke: see St John, line 59. **197 Curll:** Edmund
(1683–1747), unscrupulous bookseller. **200 Tibbalds, Moore, and
Cibber:** Lewis Theobald (1688–1744), James Moore Smythe
(1655–1723) and Colley Cibber (1671–1757), writers of limited talent, the
first and third starring at different times as the anti-hero of Pope's *Dunciad*.
230 vole: winning hand at quadrille. **238 Quadrille:** card came for

four, using forty cards, the eights, nines and tens being discarded.
249 Apollo: sun-god, patron of poetry. **253 Lintot:** Bernard
(1675–1736), bookseller. **258 Duck Lane:** area near Smithfield, given
over to second-hand book trade. **260 pastry-cook's:** remaindered books
used as pie-tin lining. **270 birthday poem:** as poet laureate, Cibber
would have written birthday verses for the King. **272 Duck:** Stephen
(1705–56), a farm labourer turned poet, taken up by Queen Caroline, who
became known as 'the thresher poet'. **274** *Craftsman:* periodical which
began in 1726 and ran for about ten years. **278 Henley:** Rev. John
'Orator' (1692–1756), cleric who wrote in support of Walpole.
281 Woolston: Thomas (1670–1733), cleric, indicted for blasphemous
'free thinking'. **300 the Rose:** Drury Lane inn. **346** *'In prin-*
ces . . .': Psalm cxlvi, 3. **378 Ormonde:** James Butler, Duke of
(1665–1745), Jacobite peer. **Oxford:** Robert Harley, Earl of
(1661–1724), formed Tory administration 1710. **381 precious life was**
ended: death of Queen Anne in 1714. **400 land of slaves and**
fens: Ireland. **410** *lifting up their heels*: see *Psalm xli, 9.* **412 cheat:**
reference to William Wood whose patent to produce Irish copper coinage
was attacked by Swift in *The Drapier's Letters.* **421 monster:** William
Whitshed (1656–1727), Chief Justice in Ireland. **424 modern Scroggs:**
Sir William (1623–83), a corrupt Lord Chief Justice compared to **old**
Tresilian: Sir Robert, who sat in judgement on Wat Tyler's followers
after the Peasants' Revolt of 1381. **426 Nor feared he God:** see *Luke xviii,*
2. **435 exile:** Swift's perspective on his life in Ireland. **449 Biennial:**
refers to the biennial convening of Parliament in Ireland. **453 Go**
snacks with: share the booty. **rapparees:** highwaymen. **478 Horace:**
first-century BC Roman satirist. **484 a house for fools:** Swift left funds
for the building of an asylum in Ireland.

p. 15 *Imitation of Part of the Sixth Satire of the Second Book of*
Horace: (first published 1728: the last eight lines have been attributed to
Pope, but the attribution has never been convincingly proven). **5 rood:**
land measure approximate to a quarter of an acre. **11 the Channel:** St
George's Channel in the Irish Sea. **15 Lewis:** Erasmus (1670–1754),
statesman. **26 levee day:** a minister's 'surgery' day. **29 ribbons blue**
and green: reference to Orders of Garter and Thistle. **65 Harley:** see
Verses on the Death, 387. **74 Pope, Gay:** see *Verses on the Death,* 47, 53.
Parnell: Thomas (1679–1718), poet and member of Scriblerus Club.
79 *inter nos*: between us. **94 will the Emperor treat:** the Emperor of
Austria who was involved in peace negotiations between Britain and
France.

p. 18 A Description of Morning: (like *A Description of a City Shower*, the poem promotes a taste for the newly-fashionable 'urban pastoral'. Both were first published in Steele's *Tatler* in 1709 and 1710 respectively). **10 kennel**: gutter. **11 smallcoal**: synonymous with coal. **13 Duns**: debt-collectors. **14 Brickdust**: reference to her coarse skin? **15 turnkey**: jailer monitoring his prisoners who had been out on 'night-release'.

p. 19 A Description of a City Shower: (see *A Description of the Morning*). **5 sink**: sewer. **14 welkin**: sky. **19 quean**: impertinent girl. **33 daggled**: spattered. **35 Templar**: student of law. **41 Triumphant Tories**: the Tories had just formed a new ministry. **43 chair**: sedan. **58 Smithfield**: London meat market. **St Pulchre's**: St Sepulchre's Church, Holborn. **59/60 Snowhill** and **Holborn Bridge**: two of London's less salubrious locations.

Poems to Stella Swift met Esther Johnson (1681–1728), whom he named Stella, when he was amanuensis to Sir William Temple in 1689. She was daughter to Temple's housekeeper, and shortly after his death in 1699, she moved to Ireland where she spent the rest of her life. The nature of Swift's relationship with 'Stella' remains obscure, although some have claimed a secret marriage. What can be affirmed, however, from the poems and the journal, are Swift's respect and tender affection. From 1719 to her death in 1728, Swift wrote regular birthday poems for Stella, five of which have been selected for this volume, together with a verse tribute to her transcription of his poetry. For readers who wish to explore further, the following would be of interest: *To Stella, Visiting Me in My Sickness*, *To Stella on Her Birthday 1721–2*, *Stella at Woodpark*, *To Stella, Written on the Day of her Birth*, *A Receipt to Restore Stella's Youth*, and the *Journal to Stella*.

p. 21 Stella's Birthday (1719): **1 thirty-four**: Swift was frequently vague about ages; Stella was thirty-eight. **5 sixteen**: see previous note; if we are to take 'first I saw' literally then Stella was eight.

p. 21 Stella's Birthday (1721): **6 Angel Inn**: probably not specific as it is a common sign. **18 thirty-six**: Stella was forty; see *Stella's Birthday (1719)*. **23 levee**: reception for visitors on rising from bed. **53 blind**: hide by smoothing over.

p. 23 Stella's Birthday (1723): **2 Stella's day**: 13th March. **13 Nine**: the Muses. **18 Jacks and Robin**: Rev. John Grattan and

John Rochfort and Rev. Robert Grattan; friends in Ireland **19 Ford:** Charles (1682–1741), friend to Swift and Stella. **Jim:** Rev James Grattan, brother to John and Robert. **20 Sheridan:** Thomas (1687–1738), cleric and schoolmaster, helped by Swift to a living although later they quarrelled. **22 *Semel'n anno ridet Apollo*:** 'Once a year Apollo laughs' (proverb). **30 Eusden:** Laurence (1688–1730), Poet Laureate from 1718. **36 to a tittle:** in just this way. **37 old Methusalem:** Methuselah, whose longevity extended to 969 years (*Genesis*, v. 27). **44 White:** William, Dean of Kilnefora. **Daniel:** Richard, Dean of Armagh. **Smedley:** Jonathan, Dean of Killala. **50 Mrs Brent:** Swift's housekeeper. **53 nine ways looking:** Mrs Brent was afflicted with a cast in the eye. **56 Saunders:** the butler. **57 Archy:** the footman. **60 Rebecca:** Mrs Dingley, Stella's companion. **62 elated:** elevated. **63 God of Winds:** Aeolus. **God of Fire:** Vulcan. **65 Bacchus:** god of wine. **74 Pluto's shades:** the underworld. **77 Robert:** the valet.

p. 25 *Stella's Birthday (1725)*: **3 lose their feet:** lose their metrical skills. **11 Sheridan:** see *Stella's Birthday (1723)*. **12 Delany:** Patrick (1685–1768), Dean of Down and close friend of Swift's. **17 The God of Wit, and Beauty's Queen:** Apollo and Venus. **23 fifty-six:** fifty-seven in 1725. **25 *forty-three*:** forty-four in 1725.

p. 27 *Stella's Birthday (1727)*: (The last of the birthday poems, and one marked by its tenderness of feeling. It was written in March 1727, and within a year Stella was dead, January 1728. The lines were first published in *Miscellanies* of 1728.) **6 spectacles:** Swift's need of spectacles was a constant source of irritation. **50 Stoics:** Greek philosophers who subscribed to an austere ethic. **53 chimeras:** grotesque, mythical monsters, hence a wild fancy. **74 Janus:** two-faced Roman god, looking forward and back.

p. 30 *To Stella, Who Collected and Transcribed His Poems*: (written 1720? published 1728). **1 pile:** large building. **4 Inigo Jones:** (1573–1652) architect who brought the Palladian style to England. **26 Conning:** study by memorizing. **34 peck:** measure of capacity. **45–46:** punishment in a house of correction. **50 Curll:** bookseller (see *Verses on the Death*, 197). **63 Stoics:** see *Stella's Birthday (1727)*, 50. **71 Maevius:** a type of mediocre poet (see Virgil *Eclogues*, III). **74 crambo:** rhyming game. **78 lost her nose:** through syphilis. **106 admire:** are amazed by. **121 Ajax:** driven to a frenzy by Pallas

Athene when he reacted with hostility to Odysseus being awarded the prize of Achilles' armour. **122 Pallas:** warrior-goddess. **136 spleen:** morose melancholy.

p. 34 _Cadenus and Vanessa_: (first published, 1726. The poem records the friendship between Swift and Esther Vanhomrigh whom he met in 1708 when he was forty and Esther about twenty. How intimate the friendship became remains open to speculation, and Swift's fanciful account of their relationship in Venus' Court of Love could hardly claim to clarify the affair). **'Cadenus'** is an anagram of Decanus, a reference to Swift's appointment as Dean of St Patrick's in 1713. **'Vanessa'** seems to be a compound of _Van_homrigh and _Essy_ (Esther). **2 Cyprian Queen:** Venus. **46 equipage:** coach. **50 toilets:** dressing rooms. **89 pent:** confined. **93 their King:** Apollo. **96 Graces:** sister-goddesses who conferred beauty. **107 _Fleta's_, Bractons, Cokes:** treatises on English law. **111 Dido's case:** for an account of Dido and Aeneas, see the _Aeneid_, books I–IV. **112 Tibullus:** Roman poet. **114 Cowley:** Abraham (1618–87) and **Waller:** Edmund (1606–87), English poets known for their love lyrics. **122 Demur, imparlance, and essoign:** legal jargon. **126 Clio:** Muse of History. **136 Lucina:** Juno, as guardian of childbirth. **155 amaranthine:** the amaranth was an immortal flower. **157 Titan:** presumably the Titan, Hyperion ie the sun. **188 Pallas:** otherwise Minerva. **250 Martial Maid:** Pallas as goddess of war. **306 Atalanta:** mythical huntress. **322 a new Italian:** opera singer. **330 fustian:** bombastic rhetoric. **367 in dishabille:** barely dressed. **372 Montaigne:** Michel Eyquem de (1533–92), French essayist. **373 Mrs Susan:** maid. **385 the Ring:** the ride in Hyde Park. **386 Mopsa:** ironic use of pastoral name (original found in Sidney's _Arcadia_); similarly **388 Corinna. 392 Phyllis:** see 386. **393 Tunbridge beau:** a dandy who haunted the fashionable spa at Tunbridge Wells. **396 rallied:** engaged in banter. **399 red:** cosmetic colouring. **417 Colbertine:** open lace-work. **422 patch:** apply a beauty spot. **431 ombre:** three-handed card game, using forty cards. **465 coadjutor:** assistant. **487 adamantine:** unbreakable. **666 complaisance:** amenableness. **681 'bite':** practical joke. **744 spinnet:** small harpsichord. **783 equipages:** fully decked out. **847 _Coram Regina prox' die Martis_:** law court Latin – 'in front of the Queen, next Tuesday'. **889 her son:** Cupid.

p. 58 _The Fable of Midas_: (first published, 1712. An expression of Swift's hostility to the corruption of the Duke of Marlborough. See also _A_

Satirical Elegy on the Death of a Late Famous General). **1 Midas:** King of Phrygia whose golden touch was granted by Dionysus. **5 codling:** hard apple. **6 pippin:** variety of apple. **12 gold-finders:** scavengers. **14 Mambrino:** King who appears in Ariosto's *Orlando Furioso.* **15–22:** referring to the charge that Marlborough was implicated in illegal dealing in army supplies. **25–32:** in a musical competition between the gods Apollo and Pan, Midas voted for Pan: his reward from the loser was a pair of asses' ears. **34 Pactolus:** river where Midas washed away his 'gift', turning the sand to gold. **45 perquisites:** casual profits. **56 plums for bays:** huge profits for poetic renown. **58 Pan:** goat-god, whose name puns on the Greek for 'all'. **71–72:** Marlborough was dismissed by an investigative committee.

p. 60 *A Satirical Elegy on the Death of a Late Famous General*: (first published in 1764 in the *Gentleman's Magazine,* although the Duke of Marlborough had died in 1722. For an earlier example of Swift's hostility, see *The Fable of Midas).* **2 old age:** Marlborough was seventy-two. **14 snuff:** burnt wick, or candle-end. **24 made them weep:** next-of-kin of his dead soldiers.

p.61 *The Furniture of a Woman's Mind*: (published 1735). **2 scarlet coat:** soldier. **7 coxcomb:** foppish fool. **14 cut and dry:** rehearsed. **19 raillery:** witty repartee. **railing:** an abusive harangue. **26** see *Verses on the Death,* 238. **28 groat:** low denomination coin. **32 patch:** beauty-spot. **43 Molly:** maid. **48 robustious:** boisterously robust. **59 Mrs Harding:** printer, widow to Dublin printer John Harding.

p. 63 *The Progress of Beauty*: (written 1719–20 published 1728). **1 Diana:** moon-goddess. The opening description is couched in extremely ambiguous terms, giving the moon the aspect of a decayed party-goer. The poem sustains this ambiguity by parodying the conventions of love-compliment in the comparison between Celia and Diana. **11 Celia:** a name from the pastoral love-tradition. **16 Strephon:** see 11. **19 front:** forehead. **40 confluents:** merging streams. **60 White lead:** used as a cosmetic and to repair china. **Lusitanian:** Portuguese. **73 Pall Mall:** fashionable street in St James's. **89 Partridge:** John (1644–1715), astrologer and self-styled prophet. **91 Cancer:** sign of the crab. **93 Gadbury:** John (1627–1704), astrologer. **95 Endymion:** beautiful youth, loved by Diana. **96 Mercury's her foe:** in hostile conjunction (mercury was also used against syphilis). **99 Flamsteed:** John (1646–1719), astronomer. **109–114:** effects of syphilis.

p. 67 *The Progress of Marriage*: (written 1722: first published 1765. The poem describes Benjamin Pratt [c. 1669–1721] who had been a contemporary of Swift's at Trinity College, Dublin. Rich and fashionable, he had been married a year to Philippa, daughter of the Earl of Abercorn, when he died.) **1 Aetatis suae:** of his age. **4 Earl:** see headnote. **7 Cyprian Queen:** Venus. **9 Graces:** see *Cadenus and Vanessa*, 96. **Muses:** nine goddesses of the arts. **11 Juno:** goddess of marriage. **13 Iris:** rainbow goddess. **15 Hebe:** handmaiden of the gods, associated with perpetual youth. **23 flourished:** ornamented. **25 pippin:** apple. **31 goal:** start of a race. **39 cheapen:** ask the price or haggle. **60 mawkish:** sickly. **86 chairmen:** carriers of sedan chair. **106 the Bath:** spa waters in Bath. **109 Achelous:** river god associated with fertility. **113 genial virtue:** power of fertility. **115 horn:** of cuckoldry. **118 boiling fountain:** springs at Bath. **128 slip:** lose the chance. **136 raffling-rooms:** gaming rooms for dice. **137 Cross Bath:** triangular baths, to the west of the Roman baths. **160 ensign:** the most junior of officers. **164 jointure:** her inheritance.

p. 72 *Strephon and Chloe*: (for publication see headnote for *A Beautiful Young Nymph Going to Bed*: for names, see note 1 of that poem, and note 2 of *The Lady's Dressing Room*). **9 nice:** discriminating. **11 humours:** fluids. **frowzy:** ill-smelling. **12 noisome:** noxious, smelly. **16 pluck a rose:** urinate. **24 dog-days:** hot, unwholesome days of July–August. **37 sword-knots:** tassels tied to the hilt. **38 billet-doux:** love letters. **clouded canes:** decorated canes. **47 *Imprimis*:** in the first place. **48 Hymen:** god of marriage who carries a torch and a veil. **49 Cyprian goddess:** Venus, whose cult flourished in Cyprus. **50 infant loves:** cupids. **51 treading:** copulating, sparrows having a lecherous reputation. **56 Hebe:** handmaiden of the gods. **59 Graces:** sister-goddesses who conferred beauty. **60 Mars in scarlet vest:** Roman god of war in uniform. **61 flammeum:** bride's veil. **62 Phoebus:** Apollo, god of music. **epithalamium:** wedding song. **64 Juno:** Roman goddess of women; female counterpart to Jupiter. **65 Luna:** personification of moon and thus associated with the goddess Diana who was patroness of midwives. **85 dyed in grain:** through and through. **88 ambrosia:** food of the gods. **100 A certain goddess:** Thetis who married the mortal Peleus and bore him Achilles. **107 Semele:** loved by Zeus, by whom she had Dionysus. **125 sage of Samos:** Pythagoras. **128 burn it blue:** give off noxious gas? **133 Carminative and diuretic:** medicines for wind and urinary problems. **168 colic:** stomach ache, brought on by pease-pudding. **181 Salerno:** reference to medical school at Salerno. **192 rouser:** loud noise. **202 amaranthine:** the amaranth was an immortal flower. **230 cut and dry:** ready-made. **238 house of ease:** lavatory. **263 scheme:** political theory. **292 Lorraine's Duke, and Prince of Greece:** puppet models of the Pretender and Alexander the Great. **302 pile:** large building. **305 bubble:** empty fool.

p. 81 *A Beautiful Young Nymph Going to Bed*: (published in pamphlet form in 1734, together with *Strephon and Chloe* and *Cassinus and Peter*). **1 Corinna:** like Strephon and Celia, one of those parodic pastoral names. **Drury Lane:** and **3 Covent Garden:** areas devoted to the sex-trade. **4 toast:** (ironically) a beauty to whom men drank a toast. **17 plumpers:** device for filling out shrunken cheeks. **30 shankers, issues:** venereal ulcers (chancres), discharges. **35 front:** forehead. **37 bolus:** large pill. **41 Bridewell and the Compter:** house of correction for prostitutes, and a prison for debtors and criminals. **43–44:** installed for sale in a sleazy inn by her pimp. **45 Jamaica:** place for transportation of criminals. **47 Fleet Ditch:** London river doubling as a sewer. **50 cully:** simple victim. **52 duns** debt-collectors. **53 rubs:** violent encounters. **59 plaster:** poultice. **63 issue-peas:** an application to stem discharges. **64 Shock:** lap-dog. **73 dizened:** decked out.

p. 83 *The Lady's Dressing Room*: (first published 1732 – frequent reprintings attest to its popularity). **2 Celia:** the name (also **Strephon**, 5) calls up the convention of pastoral love poetry, of which the whole poem is a grotesque, urban parody. **4 tissues:** rich cloth. **6 Betty:** maid. **24 lead:** white lead as cosmetic. **26 front:** forehead. **27 alum-flour:** powdered mineral. **32 whelp:** puppy. **33 gallipots:** cosmetic jars. **35 pomatum:** pomade, scented ointment. **48 frowzy:** ill-smelling, slatternly. **53 coiffs and pinners:** close-fitting cap, and the same with side-flaps. **83 Pandora:** sent by the gods, she brought with her a box containing all the ills and evils that man would suffer: the box was opened by her husband **Epimethus** (84), leaving only 'hope' inside. **98 'secrets of the hoary deep':** Milton's *Paradise Lost* II, 890–91. **110 plumped:** as we might say, 'plopped'. **126 jump:** match. **131–32:** Venus rose from the waves. **134 Statira:** heroine of Nathaniel Lee's *The Rival Queens*. **pocky quean:** pox-marked harlot. **139 clout:** rag.

p. 87 *Cassinus and Peter:* (for publication see headnote for *A Beautiful Young Nymph Going to Bed*). **1 sophs:** second-year undergraduates.

10 spleen: morose melancholy. **21 jordan:** chamber-pot. **29 doze thy pate:** become befuddled. **34 Aurora:** goddess of dawn. **35 hyps:** doleful hypochondria. **48 greater pox:** syphilis. **73 Arcadians:** inhabitants of a pastoral idyll. **80 Cerberian:** Cerberus, three-headed watchdog of Hades. **81 Alecto:** one of the three Furies. **83 Charon:** ferryman who carried the dead across the River Styx to Hades. **85 Medusa:** Gorgon whose face could turn one to stone. **88 'Avaunt – ye cannot say 'twas I':** conflated echo from Macbeth. **108 Echo:** who fell in love with Narcissus. **109 Zephyr:** personified West Wind. **112 discover:** disclose.